A Collector's
Guide to Nineteenth-Century
Jugs

KATHY HUGHES

Routledge & Kegan Paul
London, Boston and Henley

I dedicate this book with gratitude to my husband, Paul Hughes, whose help, support and patience have been unlimited

First published in 1985
by Routledge & Kegan Paul plc

14 Leicester Square, London WC2H 7PH, England

9 Park Street, Boston, Mass. 02108, USA and

Broadway House, Newtown Road,
Henley on Thames, Oxon RG9 1EN, England

Set in Linotron Caledonia
by Input Typesetting Ltd, London
and printed in Great Britain
by The Thetford Press Ltd
Thetford, Norfolk

Library of Congress Cataloging in Publication Data

Hughes, Kathy, 1926–

 A collectors's guide to nineteenth-century jugs.
 Bibliography: p.
 Includes indexes.
 1. Pitchers—Great Britain—Collectors and collecting.
2. Pottery—19th century—Great Britain—Collectors and collecting.   I. Title.
NK4695.P5H84   1985   738.3'83   85–2227

ISBN 0–7102–0302–0

Contents

Preface

Rather early in the game as a collector and a dealer, I developed an immense interest in the relief-moulded jugs which were encountered in the course of my travels. The sheer numbers and range of styles were an endless source of astonishment to me. Gradually I began acquiring them and pursuing whatever information could be gleaned from published sources. Interestingly, the more I read about pottery, the less information appeared to be available as it pertained to moulded jugs. Clearly this was a neglected field.

Yet years of experience have taught me that books which precisely identify purchased items add immeasurably to their pleasure and profit. The field of pottery is a vast and well-examined one, but there is little material on these intriguing relief-moulded jugs which were produced by the thousands during one brief fifty-year span. Admittedly, they comprise only a small part of the pottery field, but they are unique and they mirror a way of life that is gone, yet remembered fondly in these turbulent times.

This book is an attempt to place moulded jugs in historic perspective and fill that void in the store of information already published on pottery. I have attempted to carefully catalogue and identify a broad assortment of these utilitarian and decorative jugs which I hope the dealer and collector will find useful and rewarding.

I am interested in hearing from readers with any information they may have about moulded jugs. The address to write is:

Mrs Paul Hughes,
Tudor House Galleries
2900 Selwyn Avenue
Charlotte
North Carolina
28209
USA

For further information see p.138.

Acknowledgments

So many friends and acquaintances have helped me in compiling this digest that I cannot list them all. I do, however, wish to thank Mr Stephen Hughes, without whose meticulous research this book would never have been started, Mrs Sheila Warshaw, whose writing talents helped pull my random thoughts together, Miss Valerie Scott, who typed and edited my manuscript, and Mrs Sarah Latimer, Richard Riley Antiques, and Mr Carl Pearson, whose collections and knowledge were put at my disposal.

I wish also to thank Mrs Patricia Halfpenny of the City Museum, Stoke-on-Trent, Miss Margaret McFarland of Hampshire County Museum Service, Mr Robert Copeland of the Spode Museum, Mrs Joan Jones of the Minton Museum, Mr F. E. Laney of the Worcester Museum, Mrs Lynn Miller of the Wedgwood Museum, Dr Geoffrey Barnes, Mr Geoffrey Godden, Mr Peter Jackson, Sir Robert Cooke of Athelhampton, Mr Ernst Gruber, Mr Sven Gahlin, Miss Moira Thunder of the Victoria and Albert Museum and Mrs Derek Dudson.

Definition

A moulded jug is by definition any jug whose basic shape is formed by pressing wet clay into a mould as opposed to its being formed by throwing on a potter's wheel or modelled by hand. There are several ways in which the decoration of these jugs can be performed:

1 The jug can have little or no decoration other than the design of the basic shape.
2 The jug can be glazed and decorated with enamelling as was done by Ridgway in Illustration No. 27.
3 Decoration can be moulded separately from the jug and applied to the basic shape with wet clay slip. This is called sprigging and was used extensively in the first thirty years of the nineteenth century on hunt jugs and late in that century on tankard type jugs which had been thrown on a wheel.
4 The jug and its decoration can be moulded in one process. It is this latter method which was used most commonly from the 1830s through the 1870s and is what the term 'nineteenth-century relief moulded jug' generally means.

A bit of history

EARLY DAYS

From the very beginning of time, man found it necessary to devise a vessel which would contain and transport liquids. His early efforts to solve this problem resulted in the use of clay, which he found all around him, to make a primitive type of jug. Perhaps accidentally he dropped one of the early clay jugs into the fire and discovered that the heat hardened it, making it more durable.

Decoration naturally followed. Our Neolithic forebears saw fit to embellish their simple clay pieces with dots and scratches before baking them in the hot Mesopotamian sun. Moreover, archaeological finds indicate that colour decoration followed fairly soon thereafter, considerable progress in pottery making being evident before the end of the Neolithic period. The staggering number and variety of pottery pieces found across the ancient world attest to a remarkably sophisticated design technique which found its best expression in the making of urns, vases and jugs. Since all these vessels held water or wine that was shared it is no exaggeration to say that they were of communal significance and very much the centre of social and religious life.

Thus, the art of pottery making was an important feature of developing civilisation, often a barometer of the style of living prevalent at any given point in history. Because of its almost unalterable quality once it has been fired it is truly valuable as historic and archaeological evidence. Movements of people can be traced, and the layers upon layers of ancient civilisations can be documented. In Europe pottery reached its zenith during the eighteenth century when all the knowledge acquired by man was being distilled into a fine mixture expressed in the whole range of the arts. There was a veritable explosion of ideas and inventions that gave impetus to the pottery industry, particularly in England, birthplace of the Industrial Revolution.

Until the seventeenth century the only truly hard pottery was the unglazed dry red stoneware imported from the Chinese, who had found the secret of vitrifying clay much earlier than the Europeans. The rising popularity of hot drinks, such as tea and chocolate, however, provided the driving force for western countries to find the secret of making this unusually durable pottery for themselves. Success first came on the Continent. It was not long before England had the secret, and launched an industry that was to lead the world in innovations for ceramic production.

From the Neolithic age, when man in part abandoned the hunt for a more sedentary life, until the seventeenth century pottery was produced by the individual or for local markets by the resident potter farmer as a cottage industry. It was not until the early Iron Age, about 75BC, that the first pottery wheel was imported, the very first mechanisation of the craft.

The Romans brought their vast pottery-making skills to Britain. Excavation in Trent Vale, Staffordshire, has produced a Roman circular draught kiln and a type of pottery named for the area which was decorated with fine sand and gravel sprinkled on clay slip. Other excavations have produced many examples in quantity of pottery of this period.

Findings from the Saxon time, the great Dark Ages of Europe, are meagre, reflecting perhaps the general dearth of culture brought about by feudalism. However, excavations from the Middle Ages have produced a wealth of findings. Pottery was still made wherever clay was available and demand dictated, but output did start to be concentrated in the towns. William the Conqueror and his descendants ruled England. We find a record of surnames in Staffordshire such as Thomas le Throwere at Biddulph and le Potter of Audley, attesting to the fact that these men were professional potters. We know of a licence to make pottery given to William le Potter in 1348 by the Lord of Tunstall Manor. Perhaps he potted for his lord's household only, or perhaps he potted for the whole town.

From this period in addition to kilns a wealth of pitchers, jugs, cooking pots, tiles and all kinds of household pots have appeared, mostly unglazed, although a few bore an iron or copper oxide for colour. On Abbey sites throughout the North of England a ware called 'Cistercian' was found on which was used slip decoration, a process used extensively into the eighteenth century and still used to some extent today.

THE BEGINNING OF AN INDUSTRY

Recent findings strongly indicate that the second half of the seventeenth century brought a much more developed pottery industry than had previously been believed. Robert Plot in the 1680s in his book on the Staffordshire Potteries has recorded for us a detailed account of the industry at this time. He describes the centres of manufacture such as Wednesbury, Burslem and Newcastle-under-Lyme, as well as the local sources of the clay, the raw materials used, and the various processes of making, decorating and distributing pottery. His book is a veritable wealth of information about the beginnings of the industry. We see clearly from Plot that though it was a more developed industry potters still used local materials and potted for local people. They also sold their pots to travelling salesmen who carried their wares on their backs. In this way it was distributed throughout England, and a thriving export trade with the American Colonies was established.

Few seventeenth century potters can be identified with any certainty. Some large decorated dishes bear the names of Ralph, James and Thomas Toft, but it cannot be proven that these men were actually the potters. However there is a record that Thomas Wedgwood inherited in 1656 all the pottery implements which had belonged to a John Colclough.

One potter's name that stands out from the seventeenth century is that of John

Dwight of Fulham who is considered to be the father of English stoneware. He successfully produced a German type stoneware in 1677, from which most of the moulded jugs considered in this volume have evolved. Dwight developed the basic composition of stoneware and also experimented in decorative forms including applied reliefs, which forecast Wedgwood's cameo designs.

The arrival in England by 1690 of David and John Phillip Elers, was of great historical importance to the pottery industry. By 1693 they had established a factory in North Staffordshire after the closure of their London plant. There is some evidence that this move was encouraged by a legal action against the Elers by John Dwight of Fulham who claimed infringement of his patent for the manufacture of red and black stoneware. The Elers remained there in Staffordshire until 1698 by which time they had again moved, this time to Dublin, most likely in anticipation of the bankruptcy procedure which took place in 1700.

The Elers came to Staffordshire with revolutionary techniques in the use of lathes to produce a smooth surface finish to their slip cast wares. They further perfected the process for making red stoneware tea services which they copied from the Chinese yi-hsing period. It was forty years or more before these slip cast red pots were made again. Three-quarters of a century later Josiah Wedgwood, when trying to copy the red pots of Elers, commented 'we shall never be able to make the russo antico otherwise than to put you in mind of a red-pot teapot'.*

These two men like the potters before them were of an independent turn of mind who relied upon themselves and their own initiative for their success. They did not need the formal or royal patronage so avidly sought by the Continental potters. Their stern self-discipline helped dictate the responsible direction taken by pottery making in England.

Although no pieces have been found on the site, some believe that the Elers brought salt glazing to England, the process later used throughout Staffordshire which superseded faience and semi-porcelain surfaces. If so, their timing was impeccable, for it coincided with the great upsurge of the use of tea and chocolate in England. Salt-glazed surfaces were made in their thousands to be used all over Britain.

THE EIGHTEENTH CENTURY

The first half of the eighteenth century was marked by the enormous increase in the number of potteries and workers and in the areas covered by these potteries. It was a time of extensive experimentation with better ways to make the body, to glaze the surface and to decorate the pieces. The Industrial Revolution was just about to happen. The great middle class was just emerging, bringing with it the desire for, and the ability to purchase, manufactured goods of all kinds. There were over 150 potters in North Staffordshire alone who recognised the possibilities for profit in this great social happening and strove to outdo each other producing better goods to service it. Great improvements were made in the stoneware body which

* Wedgwood to Bentley, 3 March 1776.

had earlier been introduced from Germany by Dwight. Examples were generally unmarked, but most of the important potteries of the day produced them. By 1720 calcined crushed flints had been added to the body which improved whiteness, aided vitrification and made the item less likely to collapse in the firing. The added whiteness showed the new salt glaze to much greater advantage.

These eighteenth-century potters assured the triumph of British ceramics in that they were first and foremost scientists and men of business. They transmitted their knowledge to their sons, and to their sons' sons. They held both the management and the ownership of their business tightly in their own hands, so that policies could be unfettered by personality conflicts. Commerce is, and always has been, to the middle-class Englishman a prideworthy and dignified enterprise. A natural conservatism was far stronger than a desire for self-dramatisation. For the most part, constraint and consistency of design resulted. Abroad the market was starting to shift from the prerogative of the upper classes to the fulfilling of the desires of the practical middle classes, and the appeal of English earthenware, uniform, durable and aesthetically pleasing, superseded the popularity of the European designs.

1740 saw the introduction of plaster of Paris moulds reducing the dependence of the potter on the wheel and lathe and greatly increasing the number of pots any one man could produce in a day. This allowed the English potters to fill the increased demand from Britain, the Continent and indeed from America. Ralph Daniel of Cobridge is credited with introducing a plaster of Paris mould from France. This type of mould quickly replaced the old pitcher of fired-clay mould with intaglio and alabaster moulds. In addition to increasing the possible production, plaster moulds were cheaper to make, allowed far greater variety of shapes, facilitated the removal of articles from the mould, and quickly dried for more frequent re-use. Thus to those of us who are interested in relief moulded jugs, Dwight and his stoneware and Daniel and the plaster mould are two names and processes of enormous importance.

With the advent of plaster mould, two new types of pottery worker came into being, the mould maker and the slip caster. Increased importance came also to the hollow ware pressers and the model makers, particularly the latter who worked the master design in clay then passed the fired item to the mould makers for mass production.

It is important to understand the difference in the two types of moulding done by these mould makers and slip casters, that is the processes of press moulding and slip casting, so perhaps we should at this point take a minute to discuss it. In multipart press moulding a smoothed sheet of clay is pressed into each part of the mould, trimmed and the mould parts tied together. The seams are joined under pressure or smoothed together from the inside by hand or with a long tool. When the clay has dried and shrunk the mould is released and the outside of the seams trimmed. The piece may be complete or may have to be attached with liquid clay to other moulded parts to form complex objects. The piece is then ready for the next stage which may be biscuit or gloss firing.

Slip casting is done with a similar type of mould, but a more liquid clay is used. Water absorption into the mould takes place, drying the clay closest to the plaster, but leaving the excess in a liquid state. The excess is poured off, the piece removed, trimmed, and proceeds as before. Slip casting has been used alongside press moulding from the 1740s to the present but has been less popular because of the problems of making a suitable water-based slip which was not soured. This was not accomplished until the end of the nineteenth century. In general in the nineteenth century parian jugs were slip cast, while stoneware jugs were press moulded. Twentieth-century reproductions of the stoneware jugs are usually slip cast. This difference provides one with a very good method of distinguishing original nineteenth-century stoneware jugs from twentieth-century reproductions. If the inside of the jug is basically smooth with few or no indentations or recesses, press moulding was most likely used. If there are recesses inside the jug which follow the outlines of the relief on the outside, it most likely has been slip cast. It is easy to understand that the liquid clay in the slip cast process would dry to a fairly even thickness before the excess was poured out. Thus relief found on the outside would necessitate recess on the inside.

But let us go back to the mid-eighteenth century which brought other technological advances. A beginning was made in the harnessing of power by the use of watermills and windmills, greatly facilitating the grinding of the flint. Better controls were developed for the firing of pottery, and it was discovered that placing clay vessels in different parts of the oven resulted in different colours on the pattern. Ralph Shaw of Cobridge, John Mitchell of Burslem and Thomas and John Wedgwood of Burslem all played a part in these experiments.

JOSIAH WEDGWOOD AND HIS ENTREPRENEURS

The most important invention, however, was the development of creamware by the early 1760s which was perfected by the most influential name in the history of the pottery industry, Josiah Wedgwood. Creamware became the standard earthenware used by almost all the potters of the day, and its formula was never patented. It brought about the demise of white salt-glazed stoneware as the body and glaze used for so many pottery surfaces.

Queen's ware was the name that Wedgwood gave his version of creamware as it was chosen by Queen Charlotte for a tea service in 1765, bestowing royal approval upon the product.

Born 1730 of a long line of potters, Wedgwood came from a well-etablished local family of modest means. When he was nine he was apprenticed and worked in the trade all of his life. At the age of twenty-four, the young Wedgwood became a junior partner in the firm of Thomas Whieldon, a master potter, and a talented trainer of apprentices. Some of the training which stood Josiah in such good stead later was received under the tutelage of this important man.

In 1759 Josiah Wedgwood established his first independent factory at Burslem, went on to perfect Queen's ware and developed jasperware, for which he is best known. He was a great scientist and developed several devices for producing ceramics. Much of his success was due to his being a total perfectionist. For instance, he made 10,000 trial pieces in the form of small tablets of clay before he made a jasper body which pleased him. The result was a biscuit-like porcelain material, which lent itself to cameo-like decorations. The same deliberation and care went into his famous black basalt ware. He was a master potter with a high standard of craftmanship. Perhaps his most important single creation was his ceramic copy of the lovely fourth-century Cameo glass vase called the Portland Vase.

In many ways, one could call Wedgwood a modern-day businessman. He travelled all over Britain on business, absorbing information, but employed experienced sales persons who would indicate to him public preferences and habit, a primitive form of market research. He sponsored public works, which brought him much good will. He was an early member of the Society for the Abolition of Slavery, espoused freedom for the American colonies, and supported the French Revolution as a betterment to the life of the French peasant. His many friends were found among every class, showing him to be a man of the people. One of his less-publicised contributions to the industry of pottery was his campaign and personal financial contribution to the improvement of roads and the building of canals. He knew that to facilitate transport of raw materials to, and the finished produce from, Staffordshire potteries was to vastly expand the markets. He was a man of great vision.

Wedgwood insisted upon quality workmanship. Legend has it that he was known personally to break any pot with a flaw. It is said that 'This won't do for Josiah Wedgwood'* could be found written in chalk on the bench of a chastised worker. He promoted specialisation of labour, and oversaw its progress as he stomped around on his one good leg and his one wooden one.

Personally Josiah was a highly religious man who in the perspective of the day put his religious beliefs into practice in his pottery. Cancer of the jaw caused him great pain and anguish in his last few days but he never faltered in his belief that all things worked for the glory of God.

Although Wedgwood was the giant of the eighteenth-century ceramics industry, many fine potters were his contemporaries and rivals. Names such as Littler, John Baddeley, John Turner, Elijah Mayer, Charles and Ephraim Chatterley and James and Charles Whitehead successfully copied and worked to improve upon Wedgwood's processes. It is felt that history has underestimated their importance. Of particular interest to readers of this volume is the work of the Ralph Woods of Burslem, father, son and grandson, who made perhaps the first, and some say the finest, Toby jugs, examples of the development of moulded figure making in England. Early figures were made in two-part moulds and their subjects were generally from classical and mythological sources. As the century progressed, more complex moulded figures were made, drawing on literature and history to add' to the range. These figures, first cousins to moulded jugs, were made in enormous quantities in the last half of the eighteenth and throughout the nineteenth centuries.

THE INDUSTRIAL REVOLUTION

The last half of the eighteenth century saw an ever-quickening expansion of the industry with the extensive experimentation with new materials, processes, shapes and decorations. As we have seen, stoneware was followed by creamware, black basalt, jasperware, and silver, copper and resist lustres.

* Samuel Smiles in Mantoux, *Industrial Revolution*, 385.

Then, in 1753, at the Battersea enamel works the first examples of transfer printing appeared. This process brought a whole new dimension to the making of ceramics, for it offered much less expensive ways of decorating pottery. It was a product truly for the masses. The first transfer printing was done overglaze in black only and was called black-printing; but red and blue oxide-stained oils were soon used. The next step, of course, was an attempt at underglaze printing. Using glazing improvements developed by J. Greatbach, Josiah Spode from 1784 developed the technique of turning out large quantities of popular blue printed ware.

From the 1820s, brown and green underglaze prints were used on all types of table ware. Multi-coloured transfers quickly followed.

There was enormous acceptance from nearly every section of society for these transfer-printed table goods. To meet this gigantic demand, all the established potteries turned at least part of their efforts to producing them. New potteries sprang up to follow their lead. The larger companies established their own engraving works, while the smaller ones used the services of one or more of the many independent engraving establishments which opened to fill the need.

Engraving was only one of the many ancillary services and suppliers which attached themselves to the pottery trade at this time of great industrial growth. Enamelling, painting, gilding, crate making, and saggar and other kiln furniture making were performed by outside independent craftsmen for many of the potteries.

The swift expansion of the pottery trade stimulated the growth of other industries and greatly contributed to the economic well-being of the country. New sources of valuable clay were needed and found in Cornwall. Lead merchants set themselves up in clay-rich areas and provided expensive and necessary lead supplies to the potters. The enormous use of coal of the right quality in firing the kilns brought about extensive deep mining for that important raw material. Canals were dug and improved until Britain was webbed with a network of water arteries carrying raw materials to, and finished products from, the factories. Roads were built and improved for the same purpose. Partnerships were formed, dissolved and re-formed within the industry and within the interrelated industries as needs for capital ebbed and waned. The industrial revolution was in full swing. Technical knowledge started to wend its way into other parts of the world from Britain's sucessful potteries, a trend which caused some worry among the owners and management of English potteries. Factories set up in the West Indies and North America successfully hired English talent who brought with them secrets of the trade. Spies arrived from the Continent seeking the formulas for the new English products which had caused the ruin of European companies producing the outmoded faience. Some spies temporarily went to work in Staffordshire factories to learn techniques.

It was an exchange, however, for English pottery greatly benefited from the immigration of foreign workers into Britain, particularly in the decorating side of the business. In the middle of the eighteenth century two Dutchmen came to Staffordshire with the secret of enamelling followed by a number of artists and designers including the flamboyant John Voyez of figure-making fame. In 1848 the French potter, Leon Arnoux, came to work for Minton, an event that preceded a flurry of followers.

Effective systems and procedures were developed for the sales and retailing aspects of the operation as well as for the manufacturing. Factory marks, workmen's marks, patents numbers, and size numbers, were impressed, incised and imprinted on the underside of the ware to facilitate recognition, handling and selling. Illustrated catalogues were printed, sometimes in several languages. Factory processes were outlined in little booklets as advertisements for the trade. Showrooms were opened in London and the provinces with elaborate displays of dinner services and table wares. Salesmen roamed the country, bringing the products to areas not reached by the other sales operations. There were overseas warehouses, agents and salesmen. Finally, in order to unload unwanted and substandard stock, auction houses were employed.

No discussion of the development of pottery would be complete without a slight digression to touch on the ecological and sociological effects of heavy industrialisation. Potteries were concentrated in areas with rich coal deposits such as Staffordshire as it was cheaper to bring the white clay to the potteries than it was to bring the coal to the clay areas in the south. The smoke from the many kilns poured forth carbon and ash and all kinds of gaseous chemicals from the glazes into the air. Untold damage was done to the health and well-being of the workers and their families who for reasons of transportation had to live in close proximity to the factories. Sometimes entire neighbourhoods were plunged into semi-darkness. This was the flip-side of the Industrial Revolution.

Much has been written about the sociological effects of industrialisation. The situations under which the workers laboured were appalling by our standards today. The workday was very long, as much as $13^1/2$ hours not counting time for meals. Children often worked a longer day than their elders, for it was usually their job to light the fires and do the preparatory work for the potters and decorators. Often they stayed late to set up for the next day. One little boy by the name of Samuel Beard, a mould runner, in an interview in the 1840s was quoted as saying, 'I first came to work when I was five years old . . . I am twelve now.'*

Drinking was always a problem in the potteries both on the job and in the workers' free time. This, of course, was not a situation unique to the potteries and was the reason that Queen Victoria set up licensing laws. A long weekend of debauchery would be followed by long hours of work in order to catch up on wages. Wedgwood and other conscientious employers fought this problem, but many others turned a blind eye preferring to simply live with it.

Workers who were not members of the family of the owner had few if any rights and could be fired on the caprice of the owner. However the annual hiring agreement was totally binding on the employee, who faced imprisonment if he broke it.

Wages of the day cannot be called generous though they were generally better than those found in many other industries. In 1769 it is recorded that wages in Wedgwood's pottery ranged from 7 shillings a week for a grinder to 12 shillings for a gilder, although one modeller was paid £100 a year.

Please see Appendix II for statements taken from pottery workers, in 1842. These give eloquent testimonial to working conditions of that day.

* 2nd Rep. Com. Child. Emp. (430) p. 8 H.C. (1843) xiii.

THE MOULDED JUG

The recovery of the 1830s coincided with the accession of Victoria and with the emergence of the relief moulded jug as a distinct art form. Nearly every potter of that period began production of these novel containers. It was on the moulded jug alone that some designers' and potters' reputations rested.

The Victorians were in every aspect of their daily lives lovers of a sentimental expression of ideas. They inspired and appreciated these household jugs because of their sentimental, emotional, patriotic and homely themes.

Later in this chapter, we shall trace the chartable development of design which the years 1830–1880 produced, but first a brief mention of some of the companies and personalities who contributed most to the development of these jugs.

The first and disputably the most important of the potters of the true moulded jug was William Ridgway of Hanley. From about 1830 he potted press moulded jugs, mostly in a tan stoneware, but sometimes in a light green or blue. He produced jugs in their teeming thousands. Because of constant use, breakage was enormous, so that every household and pub would have a number to use and for spares. On 1 October 1835 Ridgway registered his first pattern with the public records office, under an act which protected sculptural work only from duplication. On the bottom of the vessel he impressed the words: PUBLISHED BY W RIDGWAY & CO., HANLEY, OCTOBER 1ST, 1835. This same registration was used for several designs, including Tam-O-Shanter, Morning Glories and Linen Fold. This company also operated under the names of Ridgway and Abington and of William Ridgway, Son & Company.

The firm of Charles Meigh of Old Hall Works, Hanley, came into existence in 1835 and with their stoneware jugs brought to a fine art precise relief moulding. The much-desired Apostles and Minster jugs offer testimonial to the quality of their workmanship. In 1850 they became Charles Meigh, Son and Pankhurst of the same address, and under this name continued to produce moulded wares.

Mintons of Stoke on Trent had been on the scene a long time, since 1793 in fact, before they entered the moulded jug competition. Some stoneware jugs were manufactured by them in the 1840s, but the big contribution of this fine pottery was in the moulding of parian jugs, which they produced in great quantity in the 1850s and 1860s. Whenever one finds an unmarked parian jug of high quality, it is reasonable to guess that it may have been made by Minton.

Copeland and Garret of Stoke, later W. T. Copeland, were also active in the production of parian jugs, as well as other parian table wares and figures. They too contributed some stoneware versions, but are best known for their parian. The firm came into existence in 1833 and remains today, its name having been associated with the pottery trade since 1796. The name, Masons, is most closely associated with Ironstone China, which is still being produced and enjoyed today. All the Masons jugs in this volume were made of this ironstone.

Edward Walley and Elijah Jones entered into a partnership in 1841 under the name of Jones and Walley to produce earthenware and parian. Prior to their partnership from 1831 to 1839 Elijah had operated on his own as Elijah Jones of Villa

Pottery, Cobridge. Subsequently from 1845 to 1856 Edward went it alone as Edward Walley of the same address. Thus for a total of 21 years the three firms made moulded jugs of a quality to compete with Charles Meigh. Their moulding was beautifully done, their stoneware body was smooth, and their themes were interesting. Two of their much-sought-after designs were the Good Samaritan jug and the Gipsy jug.

Quality of workmanship, design and moulding were all the hallmarks of the jugs made by Samuel Alcock and Co of Cobridge and Hill Pottery, which operated from 1828 to 1859. These jugs were potted in both stoneware and parian. Alcock are most famous for the lovely lavender and white parian jugs which they made in the 1840s and 1850s.

T. & R. Boote Limited of Burslem are best known for their contribution to the shape of jugs, for in 1847 they introduced the then new tankard outline. It was basically straight-sided with a slight taper at the top and was used intermittently by several firms until the 1870s. At this time its popularity increased and it remains to this day the most popular design for household jugs ever developed. From 1842 until 1906 Boote made earthenware, parian and tiles. Subsequent to 1906 only tile production remained and continued until the present period. Worcester, founded in 1751, is renowned for the quality of all their wares. We are interested however, only in their production of parian jugs, two marked ones of which are illustrated in this book, numbers 123 and 124. Though many parian jugs are reputed to have been made by this company in the 1850s they are a rarity today.

Perhaps the most prolific potter of jugs was William Brownfield of Cobridge. From 1850 to 1891 he registered at least 49 different designs, and endowed some of them with the most non-descriptive of names. Aston, Avon, Argos, Kent, and Lisbon all tell us nothing about what to expect for design on the jugs they represent. Most Brownfield designs were well-made and the jugs were of graceful shape. Most of the patterns were floral or geometric, though some were commemorative.

Another prolific producer of jugs, was James Dudson of Hanley, who plied his trade from 1838 to 1888. He made earthenwares, figures and jaspers both for the retail trade and for other potters.

These are only a few of the hundreds of potteries which designed, copied, and produced relief moulded jugs. It is impossible to list, much less describe, them all, but please see Appendix No. 1 for a list of all potters whose jugs are represented in this book.

PROGRESSION OF MOULDED JUG DESIGN

The development of jugs followed a fairly discernible pattern which can be readily charted, and almost all the potters moved along with these changes. Even though the potters registered their designs, and often placed their names on the bottom of the jugs, designs were frequently exactly copied by rival firms, so that often one finds the same design made by several different potters. Also patterns were freely passed around by the potters, or carried from one to the other by the artisans who moved from company to company.

A bit of history

The forerunner of the moulded jug was 'Fair Hebe', designed by John Voyez and produced over the years by various potters, such as Ralph Wood and Robert Garner. It illustrates in deep relief and very colourful glazes the story of Hebe, the Greek Goddess of Youth who offended Zeus, whom she served, by tripping and exposing herself as she filled the goblets of the God and his friends.

The early Turner jugs (circa 1780) were generally cream stoneware which had been thrown on a wheel and decorated with sprigged hunt scenes with many figures of hunters, dogs and horses set in an English landscape. The relief was usually very crisp but shallow compared to the deep moulding of the 1830s. Many jugs had a distinctive glazed band of dark blue or brown around the rim and lip. The quality of the stoneware and the crispness of the design made Turner jugs some of the most beautiful ever produced.

Then there followed an assortment of thrown jugs made by many potters in the hunting motif very similar in design to Turner's. These were generally low, bulbous, with little or no foot rim, and sculpted in very shallow sprigged relief. Minton, Wedgwood, Spode, Liverpool, Rockingham, as well as many others, all produced designs following this formula.

In the early 1830s moulded jugs came into their own as a separate art form when William Ridgway first produced his jugs 'Pan' (Illustration No. 14) and 'Tam O'Shanter' (Illustration No. 26). A distinct body style that would last for about ten years evolved which featured crisp, deep relief, low body weight, a high flaring lip, an ornate high handle, and a very pronounced pedestal foot. Except for the angular shapes of Charles Meigh (Illustration No. 45) and others, the body was round and bulging.

The scope of the ornamentation of jugs of this period was unlimited. Hunt scenes continued to be made, but to them were added drinking themes, such as Toby Filpot (Illustration No. 39), religious subjects as The Good Samaritan (Illustration No. 44), events to be commemorated as Van Amburgh the Lion Tamer (Illustration No. 32), and mythological or historical stories like 'Julius Caesar' (Illustration No. 31). Paintings, books and poems, as well as every facet of Victorian life furnished the inspiration for design of the jugs of this time.

Many famous and not so famous potteries contributed to the wealth of stoneware and earthenware vessels produced. Charles Meigh of Old Hall Works, Hanley, designed the beautiful stoneware 'Apostle' jug (Illustration No. 45) which features eight of the twelve Apostles of Christ standing in Gothic arches. A straight-sided octagonal shape was used instead of the usual bulbous one in order to accommodate this design better. T. J. and J. Mayer copied this theme at a later date with his Apostles jug. This design was used again in the unmarked Chinese figures jug (Illustration No. 71).

Minton produced many lovely jugs throughout the moulded period. The Bacchic pattern (Illustration No. 37) called 'Silenus' is one of the most deeply moulded jugs ever designed. The heads of the three satyrs moulded thereon protrude an inch from the surface, making it a jug most prone to damage. This identical theme was produced by Mason's Patent Ironstone (Illustration No. 37b) and by various other companies in ironstone, glass and silver. Perhaps Minton's most important jug was Two Drivers (Illustration No. 94), which they potted in terracotta-coloured stoneware to commemorate the advent of the train and the demise of the stage coach.

As well as copying the Silenus jug, Masons designed many jugs of their own. The two illustrated hunt jugs (Nos 54 and 55) feature large dogs and game, again in very deep relief, while Falstaff (Illustration No. 11) tells the story of this Shakespearean character, in many small figures and foliage moulded in the very shallow relief used in the earlier part of the century.

The 'Gipsey' jug (Illustrations No. 47 and 47a) registered with the Public Records Office Design Registry in 1842 jointly by Jones and Walley and Samuel Alcock shows the quality of design and execution of these fine potters. Jones and Walley produced it in stoneware, while Alcock chose the new marble-like medium developed by the British in 1842 called parian. This was a substance translucent like porcelain but with a warmer cream colouring which made it more desirable for jugs. Minton, Alcock, Worcester and Copeland developed it to a fine art and used it for great quantities of household items and figures over the years. Unfortunately, many of these wares were unmarked, making identification most difficult, but, as a generalisation, the Minton colour was less creamy and their execution of design more delicate.

While Alcock sometimes potted in stoneware, their best examples of jugs were done in parian, often in a combination of lavender and white, which became something of a trademark for them (see Battle of Acre, Illustration No. 58). Biblical stories seemed to intrigue them, as witness 'Naomi' and 'Cain and Abel' (Illustrations No. 73 and 89).

The forerunner of our present-day tankard shape was registered in 1847 by T. & R. Boote. Straight sides, which tapered slightly toward the top, replaced the bulbous body of its predecessors. The lips still flared upward, but the foot rim was eliminated. Often the body was moulded in the form of a branch of that tree. Birdnesting, which pictures a little boy climbing a tree and stealing a bird's eggs, is a most interesting example of this design (Illustration No. 83). Boote and others used this form intermittently until the late 1870s when the true tankard became the most common shape for all jugs. It has continued so until this day.

By the late 1840s a drastic change had taken place in the shape and design of moulded jugs in addition to the above Mayer design. For the most part, the bulbous shape remained, but the prominent foot had become a small foot rim, the lip was lower and less flaring, the bodyweight had started to rise, relief was more shallow and a naturalistic arrangement of plant life had replaced the figures and animals of earlier times. See 'Convolvulus' (Illustration No. 84). In these 'running patterns'* plants grew in a natural fashion as opposed to the manner in which flowers, foliage, fruit, and grain had been bunched on earlier jugs. Even design which subsequently used animals and figures would include naturally growing plant life. All the potteries followed this change and started to make jugs in the new form. See 'Paul et Virginie' (Illustration No. 107).

The naturalistic motif had another facet during these years. The entire jug would be covered by a vegetable or plant form, such as the Corncob in Illustration No.

---

* This term was used by the *Art Union Magazine* in a review of French Beauvais stoneware at the Paris Exhibition of 1844.

167 and the pine cone in Illustration No. 142. Bamboo was sometimes used to cover the body, as was basketwork and the tree trunk as before mentioned.

A very popular motif, carried over from the 1840s and continued in the 1850s, was that of the putti or amorini. These naked, sexless little children are always shown in a playful stance, i.e. climbing on garlands of flowers, pulling on a rope, dancing or playing on an instrument. See 'Vintage' by J. & M. P. Bell & Co. (Illustration No. 126).

In the mid 1850s, William Brownfield registered his first jug and went on to become one of the most prolific producers of this household item. He registered at least twenty-one different designs before the registration act of 1842 expired in 1883. Nearly all were of a similar shape: proportionally taller in relation to their girth, gently sloping inward toward the neck and flaring at the spout. It was a graceful and most pleasing shape. See 'Fern' (Illustration No. 138). Generally floral subjects were used, the commemorative 'International' (Illustration No. 161) and 'Albion' (Illustration No. 165) being two notable exceptions. 'International', registered in 1862, illustrates four fields of endeavour, science, art, music and commerce in the form of classical figures set in beaded panels. 'Albion', registered in 1863, commemorates the wedding of Princess Alexandra and the Prince Regent, who became Edward the Seventh. The more bulbous 'Albion' departs from the Brownfield shape in order to more properly display the various coats of arms which it bears.

British potters exported great quantities of their jugs to the United States and designed many of their wares especially for that market. Slavery (Illustration No. 112) tells the story of *Uncle Tom's Cabin* by Harriet Beecher Stowe, as Tom is auctioned and Little Eva is carried off by the angels. George Washington (Illustration No. 132) commemorates American Independence from England as it shows the figures of George Washington and Martha set among the draped flags of the thirteen colonies.

In the next important change which took place in the development of moulded jugs, the 'free running' naturalistic look of plants was replaced by more formal, stylized flower and foliage moulded in very shallow relief. Often the background was finely stippled, a method of covering up defects. See 'Argos' registered by Wm Brownfield (Illustration No. 168). These were the jugs of the 1860s with their small foot rim, high body weight, flat rim and spout, and handle hung well below the rim.

A natural progression from stylized plants took place in the advent of the jugs of true geometric design in the late 1860's. See 'Cashmere' (Illustration No. 176). Also, about this time, the influence of the Greek Revival Movement was felt in the design of jugs, as well as in all art forms of the period. See Medallion and Swags (Illustration No. 173).

In the middle of the 1870s, Europe rediscovered Japan and all things Japanese. Every type of ceramics was influenced by this design from the East which featured random shapes and sprays of plants, and was the inspiration for the new movement called 'Art Nouveau'. See Japanese Sprays (Illustration No. 196).

The birth of Art Nouveau coincided with the death of the moulded jug. The new tankard shape which Wedgwood, Adams and others used so successfully with applied motifs became the overwhelmingly predominant design from this date forward. See Dancing Hours (Illustration No. 201).

Whatever the subject, the design or the period, jugs were executed in a suitable clay that enhanced the effect and added to their three-dimensional artistic quality. The medium chosen, earthenware, stone or parian, was generally carefully pressed into the master mould or else mixed with sufficient water to pour into place. Although most of the jugs were made in white or tan stoneware with a smear glaze, quite a large number came in a variety of other colours and glazes. However made, all are readily distinguishable by their relief designs and characteristic shapes.

Some jugs bear metal lids which add enormously to their interest, although the lids are frequently found missing with only little holes to mark that a lid was once there. Sometimes jugs with holes never actually had a lid, perhaps due to an oversight on the part of the potter. Often there were many different sizes for each pattern, allowing the purchaser to assemble sets which could be used and displayed together.

Clearly these charming reminders of life in Victorian England offer endless choices and are a must for the pottery collector seeking a comprehensive collection. These moulded jugs blazed briefly in the history of pottery making, yet remain an important link in that chain of work stretching from the dawn of history to the modern age.

A little about marks

Over the years potters have marked their wares in several different ways. The very early jugs were either unmarked or merely marked with the maker's name.

In 1835 the 'Published by' mark started to appear on the bottom of moulded jugs. Under the law this mark protected the design of the shape or ornamentation of pottery, as well as of other manufactured goods. Jugs so protected carried a mark such as the following:

Published
As the Act Directs
June 20, 1834 by
Machin & Potts
Burslem, Staffordshire

In 1842 a new law came into effect which gave three years' protection to thirteen classes of items registered with the Registrar of Designs. Pottery was assigned class number IV. In the Public Records Office in Kew are large books containing sketches or photographs of all jugs so registered between the passage of the law in 1842 until the new law in 1883. Each picture is assigned a registration number from which the manufacturer and date of registration can be traced. In this volume, when specific dates are assigned to a jug, they are the dates on which the jugs were registered, not necessarily the dates of production.

Today we often can determine the manufacturer and date of registration for ourselves by deciphering the registration diamond which is either impressed, embossed or printed on the bottom of some jugs. A code of letters and numbers as indicated in the following table reveals this valuable information.

This table is taken from Leaflet 15 of the Public Records Office. The Crown Copyright was reproduced by permission of the Controller of Her Majesty's Stationary Office.

DIAMOND REGISTRATION MARKS

YEAR CODE

1842 X	1856 L	1870 C	
1843 H	1857 K	1871 A	
1844 C	1858 B	1872 I	
1845 A	1859 M	1873 F	a class
1846 I	1860 Z	1874 U	b year
1847 F	1861 R	1875 S	c month
1848 U	1862 O	1876 VEE	d day
1849 S	1863 G	1877 P	e bundle
1850 VEE	1864 N	1878 D	
1851 P	1865 W	1879 Y	a class
1852 D	1866 Q	1880 J	b day
1853 Y	1867 T	1881 E	c bundle
1854 J	1868 X	1882 L	d year
1855 E	1869 H	1883 K	e month

—1842-67—

—1868-83—

NOTES

(i) In 1857 the letter R was used 1–19 September.

(ii) In 1860 the letter K was used for December.

(iii) From 1 to 6 March 1878 the following mark was issued:

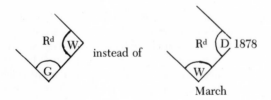

instead of

March

MONTH CODE

January	C	July	I
February	G	August	R
March	W	September	D
April	H	October	B
May	E	November	K
June	M	December	A

In addition to these two types of marks, names of potters, marks of potters, and names and numbers of patterns were often incised, impressed or printed on the bottom of the jugs.

Finally, there are a variety of numbers and letters appearing either with or without the above marks. Generally the impressed numbers 2, 3, 4, 6, 12, 18, 24, 30, 36, 42, 48, 54, 60, are size numbers. They indicate the number of units which would fit on to a potter's workboard measuring 6 feet × 11 inches or into a warehouse basket. Thus, the smaller the impressed number, the larger is the jug and vice versa. Seldom, however, was a number used for jugs larger than 42.*

Other numbers, especially large ones, are pattern numbers used by the potter to designate different designs. See 'Babes in the Woods', number 59 (Printed No. 143).

Fractional numbers usually give the date on which the jug was actually produced, a date often different from the date of registration of the design. Thus 1/48 would mean that this jug was made in January of 1848.

Other numbers and letters may indicate a date code which was used by the company, names of potters or glaziers, or any other information which the company chose to record.

* Please consult a good ceramics marks book for complete information on marks, makers, and British Patent Office registration dates.

A word on reproductions

With moulded jugs, as with any field of collecting, honest copies as well as dishonest fakes have been made through the years, right up to today. Generally speaking, it takes little knowledge to distinguish the modern from the Victorian because of the vastly superior moulding and detail of the latter. Also, many reproduction jugs are clearly marked on the bottom with an identifiable manufacturer's mark which can be traced through any good ceramics marks dictionary.

One very interesting group of reproduction jugs was produced in the 1920s by Portmeirion Potters Ltd of Stoke on Trent. The following is an excerpt from a small brochure which this company put out at that time:

> After the 1870's the moulded jugs fell out of favour. The moulds were put away and forgotten, the firms that had made them often changed hands or went out of business. As time passed the original moulds were still in existence. Recently, however, Susan Williams-Ellis, Portmeirion Potteries' Designer Chairman, was rummaging in a distant and long-disused attic at the works in Stoke, struggling through piles of Moulds for every sort of forgotten or depressing utensil: Bleeding Basins, giant Water Filters, Bed Pans – when she came on a soot covered heap of roughly cylindrical objects. What they were could hardly be seen under the dust and dirt of maybe ninety years. Miss Williams-Ellis brushed away at them and soon emerged triumphant but completely black with sooty grime, clasping the first of an important cache of over fifty Victorian Jug Moulds. A lengthy period of research and sorting followed. There was no indication which Jug had which handle and these latter were often several unlabelled parts. It meant piecing them together, as well as scouring Antique Shops and Museums and consulting numerous books to identify them and see how they were supposed·to be put together. At last, however, a unique range of these historic and fascinating Jugs has been assembled. A special technique of manufacture has been developed to reproduce the old 'parian' porcelain body in which they were made and to preserve the full sharpness of the original fine modelling.
>
> The Jugs at present in production are: Hannibal (5), Punch (5), Pilgrim (5), Cable (3), Dancing Cupids (3), Apostles (6), Distin Family (3) and Volunteer Rifles (3). The figures in brackets indicate the number of sizes available.

A letter to Portmeirion Potters asking for any information available on these reproduction jugs, produced this reply:

[18]

A word on reproductions

Enclosed you will find a photocopy of a gift leaflet we used to produce and you will see 3 sizes of Antique Jugs we used to produce. All the items in respect of moulded jugs were all produced at one time but this is a very long time ago and we have no record of their names. Eventually we only produced two types of moulded jugs, Antique Jug which is shown on our leaflet and a Water Cable Jug but regretfully after investigating the availability of these two jugs, I was told that we are unable to supply since all our stocks have been completely disposed of.

Although no Portmeirion reproduction jug has come to hand, the jugs were, in fact, clearly marked with the name of the potter, according to a present-day employee. Those who have actually seen examples of the jugs state that the glazes used are so unlike those used on the originals as to be easily identifiable as reproduction.

The Van Amburgh jug (Number 32 in this digest) was reproduced by Arthur Wood Potteries Ltd. The reproduction is clearly marked both with the manufacturer's name and 'made in England'.

Another large producer of modern moulded jugs is Burgess and Leigh, Ltd of Burslem, whose Middleport Pottery potted earthenwares from 1889. From 1930 the name 'Burleigh Ware' was used on very bright, colourful, nostalgic jugs, many of them Dickensian in motif. All of these are clearly marked with a printed 'Burleigh Ware'. This mark plus the bright glazes used protect the buyer from any confusion as to the age of the jugs.

Some moulded jugs are being made today with a printed mark on the bottom, '18th Century Stoneware Jug'. No potter's name is incorporated in the mark. These items are invariably new. To date no Victorian jug has appeared with a mark indicating the century in which it was produced. While these jugs copy the design of early ones, the mark is again the buyer's protection.

Unfortunately, reproduction jugs are being produced with no mark at all. With these, the high glazes and bright colours must be used for warning of modern manufacture.

The words 'England' or 'Made in England' on the bottom of the stoneware usually indicate a date of production after 1891, for in this year the United States passed a law which required all imported goods to be clearly marked with the country of origin. Thus the English potters began at this time to use the word 'England' on their wares, which today gives us a lovely clue as to the age of the item.

One final word of warning, although the manufacturer may clearly mark his jugs, those who choose to deceive are perfectly capable of filing off the original potter's mark, thus eliminating this clue to age.

From 1847 through 1858 an American firm trading under the names of Julius Norton, J. Norton and J. E. Norton successively produced at least 16 designs of moulded jugs which were copied directly from the English originals. Their products were called Bennington Ware, named from the Vermont town in which they were located. In addition to the copied motifs, some original designs (Corn Husk and Cascade patterns) were produced.

The moulding of these copied jugs was of very high quality making them quite difficult to identify unless a potter's mark was used. Unfortunately only about one-fifth of the Bennington Ware was so marked.

Please note the following list of known Bennington copies of English moulded jugs:

'Gipsey' (sic.) by Jones and Walley and by S. Alcock called Good Samaritan by Bennington (Illus. No. 47, 47a)

Infant Samuel by T. & R. Boote called 'Apostle' by Bennington (Illus. No. 79)

Birdnesting by T. J. & J. Mayer (Illus. No. 83)

'Nymphea' by W. T. Copeland called 'Lily Pod' by Bennington (Illus. No. 103)

'Willie' by Wm Ridgway and Co. (Illus. No. 105)

'Paul et Virginie' by T. J. & J. Mayer (Illus. No. 107)

Ivy Leaf by Samuel Alcock (Illus. No. 115)

Grinning Bacchus, potter unknown (Illus. No. 119)

'Babes in the Woods' by Cork and Edge (Illus. No. 129)

Sleeping Beauty, potter unknown called 'Spinning Wheel' by Bennington (Illus. No. 144)

Wheatsheaf, potter unknown (Illus. No. 145)

'Harvey', potter unknown (Illus. No. 160)

Pineapple by Minton (Illus. No. 184)

Ivy by Minton (not illustrated)

Cherub and Grapes by Wedgwood (not illustrated)

Love and War by Samuel Alcock (not illustrated)

In his book *Bennington Pottery and Porcelain*, Mr Richard Carter Barret illustrates all of the above jugs. Of particular interest is his comparison as to design and shape of the Bennington versions to their English counterparts.

Checklist for buying

When buying Victorian moulded jugs, please check the following:

A   Look for fine, distinct moulding.
B   Avoid highly glazed and brightly coloured jugs. (Please note the exceptions as recorded in this digest.)
C   Look for signs of wear, especially on the bottom to indicate age.
D   Avoid jugs with:
    (a) 'England' on the bottom.
    (b) Marks of companies not in production before 1890. Use any good ceramics marks dictionary.
    (c) Any mark stating '18th Century Jug'.
    (d) Chips – check especially on foot rim, lip and handle.
    (e) Cracks – the worst kind of damage since the jug is no longer watertight.
    (f) Restoration – There is no reason not to buy a restored jug if the restoration does not bother you, and as long as you know that it has been restored. Jugs should be marked 'Restored' wherever applicable. If not marked, ask for a receipt stating that it is unrestored. An ultra-violet light will reveal any new glaze the jug has been given. You can check for restoration yourself by checking all vulnerable areas carefully with eye or magnifier, thumping endangered areas (you should hear a click rather than a dull thump), and biting the foot and lip rims (restored areas will have a softer feel to the teeth).

There is no foolproof guide in buying. However, the more you look, touch and compare, the more confident you will become in your ability to differentiate between the Victorian and the modern. Eventually you will come to spot a modern jug as being obvious, even sitting on the shelf.

Information on jugs

Information on jugs is given in the following way.

Name of jug

Maker Date

Description of jug and other relevant information

Height: in inches
Description of mark, including precise lettering or arrangement in bold type
Name of the collection or agency who supplied photograph if not the author

Digest of jugs

Jug titles given by the potter will be in quotation marks. Titles without quotation marks were given by the author or taken from other books.

1
'Fair Hebe'
Robert Garner of Foley Fenton
c. 1788

Designed by John Voyez, produced in earthenware by Ralph Wood and various other potters for whom Voyez worked, this was the grandfather of nineteenth-century moulded jugs. It depicts Hebe, the Greek Goddess of youth, whose job it was to fill the goblets of Zeus. The jug takes the form of a log with Hebe and a lover in deep relief painted in underglaze colours of green, blue and brown.

Height: 8 inches
Impressed: **RG** (for Robert Garner)
Impressed: **6**
Collection: Mr and Mrs Ray Latimer

2
Pratt Type Jug
Unknown c. 1790

Another forerunner of the moulded jug hey-day. These earthenware jugs usually bore portraits of celebrities or caricatures of eighteenth-century men. This unmarked example showing a young man in an arch is typical of the soft underglaze greens, golds and browns used by Pratt and his contemporaries.

Height: 5½ inches
Unmarked

3
Hunt Jug
John Turner of Lane End
c. 1800

Stoneware made by adding ground stone to the basic earthenware was patented by John Turner of Lane End. For a very few years until 1806, he produced a quality of moulded stoneware never excelled, due to the special stone which he used from the property of the Marquis of Stafford. Bankruptcy ensued when he no longer had access to the Marquis' stone. The body of this prized Turner Hunt Jug is cane coloured with a dark brown top. The figures are sprigged in shallow relief.

Height: 7½ inches
Impressed: **TURNER**
Collection: Mr and Mrs Ray Latimer

4
Satyr Mask Jug
Thomas Harley of Lane End c. 1805

These early Satyr mask jugs were produced by Harley, often in lustre, always in bright, cheerful colours. Sometimes he used one dark bearded mask, sometimes a mask head on three sides. This single mask example is done in bright underglaze yellow which is the rarest of the colours used at that time.

Height: 5 inches
Unmarked

Height: 7 inches
Unmarked

5
Marblized Classical Jug
Liverpool Hurculaneum c. 1805–1810

Liverpool Herculaneum produced a number of wares made to look like marble, an expensive material even then. This lovely jug made in buff-coloured marblized stoneware combined sprigged classical figures and angels in shallow relief, a motif popular at this time.

6
Hunt Jug
Spode c. 1810

A small cream coloured jug with dark blue top. There is a basket-weave motif on the base and hunt figures on a stippled background. It has been turned and thrown on a wheel then sprigged and is typical of the early Hunt Jugs which preceded the true moulded jug period.

Height: 3 inches
Impressed: **Spode**

7
'Oriental'
Unknown c. 1810

A blue grey earthenware jug with Mason type octagonal body. Sprigged classical figures adorn each panel, fuchsia blossoms and leaves the top. The Hydra handle is in the form of a serpent. Why a classical motif should be called 'Oriental' is anbody's guess.

Height: 5¹/₂ inches
Impressed: **Oriental**

Height: 8 inches
Impressed: Godden's Wedgwood Mark
    No. 4074

9
Coronation Jug
Unknown c. 1820

This light-weight earthenware jug was issued in 1820 to commemorate the Coronation of George IV. The white lead glazed body is covered with the three feathers of the Prince of Wales, which are moulded in shallow relief, and the jug is highlighted with a band of brown.

Height: 7½ inches
Unmarked
Courtesy of Halcyon Days

8
Hunt Jug
Josiah Wedgwood c. 1810

A very finely moulded hunt scene surrounds the bowl of this white stoneware jug, complete with sprigged horses, riders, dogs, fences and trees. The bottom is fluted, the top banded in deep blue. This is a very fine quality Wedgwood jug.

10
The Kill
Phillips & Bagster c. 1820

Heavy squat tan stoneware jug depicting the killing of a boar by dogs on one side and of a stag by a lion on the other. Hop vines circle the top. This is definitely not a jug for delicate sensitivities. The interesting feature here is the handle in the shape of a greyhound dog, again making the jug very vulnerable. There is a popular collecting field today composed only of items with animal handles.

Height: 8¹/₄ inches
Impressed on the collar of the dog: **PHILLIPS & BAGSTER**
From the Morpeth Collection

11
Falstaff* Jug
Masons c. 1830

A tan ironstone jug ornately decorated with figures, including a rotund little man with antlers on his head representing Shakespeare's Falstaff. He is flanked by two ladies, dogs, stags, castles and foliage. This may be one of the 'Stone figured jugs' illustrated in Mason's Sale Catalogue of 1822. It was in July of 1813 that Charles James Mason, son of Miles Mason, took out the patent to continue the production of the world-famous Mason's Ironstone pottery. The patent called it 'A process for the improvement of the manufacture of English Porcelain' – a mis-statement, for it definitely was not porcelain, but rather opaque earthenware. Mason's ironstone is made today. This jug has also been found in white.

Height: 5¹/₂ inches
Printed: Godden's Mason's Crown Mark
No. 2528
Mason's Patent Iron stone China

* It has also been claimed that the central figure on this jug represents the Celtic God Cernuccus.

Height: 3½ inches
Impressed: **15**

12
Resting Deer
Unknown c. 1830

Three deer rest in the brush while a fourth is pursued by a hunter and his two hounds on this tan stoneware jug. The scalloped rim is a departure from other jugs of the period but forecasts the jugs of the mid-1830s.

Height: 5¾ inches
Unmarked

14
'Pan'
William Ridgway & Co. c. 1830

Another Bacchic jug, this time by Ridgway. It must have been made in prolific numbers for it is one of the easier jugs to find. Two masks of Bacchus, the Greek God of Revelry, are set against scrolls, acanthus leaves, and stylized anthemions on a tan stoneware body. A bust of Pan with pipes is moulded into the handle. This jug seems to have been made in sets of many graduated sizes. A most interesting find was of an Italian copy of the 'Pan' design. A small factory

13
Hunt Jug
Probably Rockingham
Swindon, Yorkshire c. 1830

The early works of this pottery were usually unmarked. This example of a thrown Rockingham shows sprigged hunt scenes on a cane coloured background. The prominent feature is the lovely serpent handle and spout. A similar jug is in the Victoria and Albert Museum. This has also been found in all white.

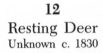

called Doccia, located near Florence, produced it in the late nineteenth century using multiple bright-coloured glazes. On the bottom was found the Doccia blue mark, a crown over a capital N.

Height: 7¹/₂ inches
Embossed: Godden's Ridgway
   Anchor & Vase Mark No. 3260

15
Gothic
Josiah Wedgwood c. 1817

Josiah Wedgwood was world famous for the development of Jasperware and creamware, or 'Queensware'. Here is a creamware jug with six blue classical figures standing in Gothic arches. The figures have been sprigged and stand above an arched footrim. This is Wedgwood's pattern number 958 and is found in the 1817 catalogue for that company.

Height: 6¹/₂ inches
Impressed: Godden's Wedgwood Mark
   No. 4074

16
Hunt Jug
Minton c. 1835

A large dark green stoneware jug, an unusual colour for jugs of this period, ornately sculptured with hunt scenes of dogs, horses and men in foliage. The relief is shallow as in hunt jugs of the early 1830s.

Height: 7¹/₂ inches
Embossed: Godden's Minton Mark No.
   2690 with pattern No. 107 inside
   cartouche

17
Hunt Jug
Unknown c. 1830

Another typical hunt scene on an earthenware body, glazed inside. The light lime-coloured glaze is most unusual; the nine dogs and three men on horseback are in shallow but crisp relief. This jug is thrown on a wheel and sprigged.

Height: 4½ inches
Impressed: **36**

18
Cottage
Unknown c. 1830

This early jug is hexagonal in shape with a cut-away foot and depicts a cottage with ivy vines on its thatched roof. The earthenware body is brown with lustre glaze. It was widely reproduced in late Victorian times but, though rarely marked, these jugs are easily distinguished from the early ones by their much brighter colours. Also found in many other combinations of colours.

Height: 4 inches
Unmarked

19
Classical Figures
Unknown c. 1830

Three groups of sprigged classical figures in white relief surround this bulbous cane-coloured stoneware jug. The neck topped by a long narrow spout bears a wreath of grape-vines, the bottom forms a basket. There is a white embossed chrysanthemum type mark which to date has not been identified. This jug has been thrown on a wheel.

Height: 6½ inches
Embossed: Chrysanthemum inside a
circle with the number **16** in the
middle
Courtesy of Richard Riley Antiques

19a
Unidentified Mark on
Jug No. 19

20
'Rev John Wesley'
Staffordshire Potteries c. 1830

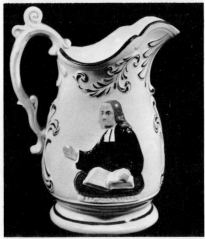

There is a figure of the Reverend John
Wesley (1703–1791), founder of the
Methodist Church, in his black
preacher's robe on each side of this white
earthenware jug. The piece is heavily
glazed and trimmed in blue and green
enamel overglaze.

Height: 8½ inches
Unmarked

21
Winged Lion and Cherub
William Ridgway c. 1830

Mask spouts were popular all through
the moulded jug era. This Ridgway
design is a Greek volute crater beneath
a finely moulded mask spout. Applied
figures of Cherub, winged lion and
foliage surround the bowl. Stoneware
was used with a brown smear glaze, and
it has been thrown on a wheel and the
figures sprigged.

Height: 5¾ inches
Unmarked, but one is to be found in the
V & A

22
'Robert Burns'
Machin & Potts 20 June 1834*

Robbie Burns and his poems were a
favourite theme in the mid-1830s, as
shown in this jug. There is a bust of
Robbie under a very exaggerated mask
spout and a scene of Tam O'Shanter on
either side. The projection of the mask
made this jug very vulnerable to
damage, thus it is rare and difficult to

find in good condition. The body is all cream with a white bust of Burns.

Height: 6¼ inches
Impressed within a cartouche:
Published
As the Act Directs
June 20, 1834 by
Machine & Potts
Burslem, Staffordshire

* An exact date given as above indicates the day on which a design was registered with the Patent Office, not necessarily the date on which this jug was produced.

23
Coral
Elijah Jones, Cobridge
1 September 1835

Twining coral covers a low tan stoneware body.

Height: 4½ inches
Impressed: **Published by**
E Jones Cobridge
Sept 1, 1835
Godden's Mark No. 2213
Courtesy of Richard Riley Antiques

24
The Kill
William Ridgway & Co.
1 October 1835

Ridgway realistically depicts a lion killing a deer and a wild boar fighting with several dogs. This is a low, fat, tan stoneware jug with a handle in the shape of a sleek greyhound dog. Hop vines encircle the neck. The motif is very similar to the earlier Phillips & Bagster jug No. 10. Also seen in tan.

Height: 6½ inches
Impressed: **Published by**
W. Ridgway and Co.
Hanley
Oct 1, 1835
From the Morpeth Collection

unmarked. Ridgway was to become perhaps the most prolific producer of moulded jugs in the 1830s and 1840s.

Height: 6 inches
Unmarked

25
'John Gilpin'
William Ridgway & Co. c. 1835

The scene from William Cowper's (1731–1800) poem 'John Gilpin' depicts John riding his uncontrolled horse between home and pub, past family and friends. The horse's head is on the handle. A ribbon bears the quotation 'Stop, Stop, John Gilpin, here is the house'. A small jug of light blue earthenware produced by William Ridgway but

got — blue — cracked no lid.

26
'Tam O'Shanter'
William Ridgway & Co.
1 October 1835

In the mid-1830s, the moulded jug came into its own with a distinct body style which would last for about ten years. Crisp and often deep relief decorated jugs with low bodyweight, high flaring lips, ornate high handles and a distinct foot. Except for the angular shapes of

Charles Meigh and a few others, the body was round and bulging. This tan-glazed stoneware jug pictures on one side, Tam O'Shanter of the poem, 'Bousin at the Nappie' by Robert Burns (1759–1796), drinking with his three friends at the pub. The other side portrays him on his horse fleeing from the witches. The smaller size jugs have only one witch, the larger ones have two as are found on this jug. Also to be found in tan, blue and light green.

Height: 11 inches
Impressed: **Published by**
　　　　　Wm. Ridgway and Co.
　　　　　　Hanley
　　　　　October 1 1835
Godden's Mark No. 3302

'Published by' means the jug was registered to protect it from duplication. This protection applied only to cast or press-moulded items portraying human or animal forms. However, some 'published by' marks have been found on later reproduction jugs bearing floral and other motifs. The early acts of Parliament in 1787, 1789 and 1794 gave only three months protection to design and pattern. The 1839 Design Copyright Act increased this to 12 months while the 1842 Designs Act increased it to three years.

From the Morpeth Collection

27
Morning Glories
William Ridgway and Co.
1 October 1835

got so repo...

Morning Glories mark a departure for Ridgway jugs of this period as the flowers are enamelled on top of a bluish-mauve glazed stoneware body instead of being in relief. The 1 October 1835 Tam O'Shanter registration was used for this jug as well as for the Linen Fold design. Please see Nos 26 and 28. Figures have been removed and flowers substituted. Ridgway made several items in this bluish-mauve glaze with enamel, which were highly valued at the time and today are very rare.

Height: 7 inches
Impressed: **Published by**
W. Ridgway & Co.
Hanley
Oct 1, 1835
12
Godden's Mark No. 3302

28
Linen Fold
William Ridgway and Co.
1 October 1835

Another Ridgway Tam O'Shanter (see Illustration No. 26) and registration, but with a linen fold design, so popular in wood carvings of the period. A simple but very elegant design used on a smear-glazed stoneware body.

Height: 6½ inches
Impressed: **12** (size)
Published by
W. Ridgway & Co.
Hanley
Oct 1, 1835
11

29
Many Masks and Scrolls
Staffordshire Potteries
c. 1835

There is an unusual design in relief on the bottom of this blue glazed earthenware jug. It is not a mark but simply a decoration (see illustration No. 29a). On the body there is a busy all-over floral design containing many masks and flowers and two masks on the spout.

Height: 7 inches
Unmarked

29a
Design on the bottom of jug No. 29

30
Vertical Leaves
Elijah Jones, Cobridge
1 September 1838

Five large vertical leaves climb a tan stoneware body.

Height: 7 inches
Impressed: Published by
E. Jones
Cobridge
Sept 1, 1838
Courtesy of Richard Riley Antiques

got good condition

31
'Julius Caesar'
Charles Meigh 1 November 1839

For only 14 years between 1835 and 1849, Charles Meigh of Old Hall Works, Hanley published and produced some of the most interesting designs of the entire moulded jug era. His quality of execution was excellent. This example, taken from an engraving L. P. Boitard made from a drawing by a man named Stevenson, depicts Julius Caesar landing his troops in Britain, and Boadicea, the Queen of the Iceni Tribe, rallying her troops. The ornate design is in shallow relief on a tan-glazed stoneware body. A metal lid adds to the interest of this quality jug.

Height: 7½ inches
Impressed inside a laurel wreath:
Nov. 1st, 1839
Published by C. Meigh
Hanley
Julius Caesar
24
From the Morpeth Collection

the time in which he lived.

Height: 8¼ inches
Unmarked

33
'Elizabethan'
Elijah Jones 1 July 1840

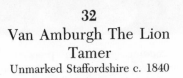

32
Van Amburgh The Lion Tamer
Unmarked Staffordshire c. 1840

Another animal handle jug, this time a lion standing on a bulbous light-blue glazed earthenware body. The famous American lion tamer, Van Amburgh, stands surrounded by six lions and five heraldic shields. His Roman tunic belies

Eight panels formed by the octagonal shape of the jug enclose Elizabethan designs around the bowl. A small bird alternates with a bird with a human head

(called 'harpie') in the panels around the neck. The jug is made of tan stoneware.

Height: 9 inches
Impressed: Godden's Mark No. 2213 in an embossed circle

34
Hannibal
Unknown c. 1840

This green stoneware jug reminds one of Charles Meigh's 'Julius Caesar' with its many warring figures. It is set in tropical surroundings and a large elephant carrying soldiers and arms stands out on each side. The scene is believed to be Hannibal and his army.

Height: 6¹/₂ inches
Unmarked
From the Morpeth Collection

35
The Wedding
Minton c. 1840

A wedding procession proceeds on horseback complete with bride, groom, flower children, dogs and guests around the body of this soft blue-green stoneware jug. The figures are crisply moulded in shallow relief topped by a floral design around the rim.

Height: 8¹/₄ inches

Impressed:
> Godden's Mark No. 2690
> Impressed inside a cartouche:
> **No. 130 M 6** (Star)

36
Gypsy Encampment
Unmarked Staffordshire c. 1840

A goat handle completes this group (Nos 10, 24, 32 and 36) of animal-handled jugs. As in No. 32, a light-blue glaze has been applied to an earthenware body from one of the Staffordshire potteries, perhaps the same factory. The scene is of a gypsy encampment and is repeated on the other side.

Height: 9 inches
Unmarked
Collection: Mr and Mrs R Latimer

37
Silenus*
Minton c. 1831

Many companies produced this Bacchic pattern called 'Silenus' including

Minton, Mason, Spode plus Continental companies copying the English design. The latter have been found complete with traces of gilding. The jug pictured is a marked Minton with a Silenus group of three in extremely high relief on each side. Grapevines adorn the green stoneware body and twine around the handle. Also found in dark green. Stephen Green also made an early version in brown stoneware. (A mug using this identical design was produced by Minton. See illustration No. 37a.)

Height: 6½ inches
Impressed: Godden's Minton Mark No. 2690
Impressed inside a cartouche: **16**
From the Morpeth Collection

* This jug has also been called Baccha or Bacchus.

This design is said to have been introduced by Minton in 1831. The angular crown mark on the bottom of this Mason example, however, would seem to indicate a much later date of production.

Height: 10½ inches
Printed: Godden's Mason's Mark No. 2528

37a
Silenus Mug
Produced by Minton

37c
Silenus
Possibly Sowerby or
Davidson Glass c. 1870

37b
Silenus
Masons Ironstone c. 1845

Masons Ironstone has used the Silenus design identical to Minton in an almost identical shade of grey-green stoneware.

The Silenus motif jug was producd in silver and glass, as well as in stoneware, parian and porcelain. This small example in white slag glass is quite unusual.

Height: 3 inches
Unmarked

38
Ox Cart and Grapes
Unknown c. 1840

An ox cart heavy laden with grapes is flanked by three men harvesting the grapes. Abundant fruit and vines cover the balance of the tan stoneware jug. Charles Meigh made many designs highly reminiscent of this one.

Height: 7 inches
Unmarked
From the Morpeth Collection

39
Toby Filpot
Unknown c. 1840

A deep relief tan stoneware jug depicting Toby Filpot against a background of

grapevines. Toby holds his mug far out, making it an almost irresistible target for breakage. Though the jug has been moulded in two halves, the arms and perhaps the head have been moulded and applied. Authorities differ as to the origin of the term 'Toby Filpot' or 'Toby' jugs but, according to Messrs Rackham and Reed in *English Pottery*, they relate to Toby Filpot, the subject of a song called 'The Brown Jug', a skilful adaptation from the Latin of the humanist physician Geronimo Cervaltio (1507–1574) written by the Rev. Francis Fawkes and published in 1761. It was probably an engraving with these verses inscribed beneath which the potters originally used for their composition.

This tan unglazed rough stoneware body is sometimes called 'drab ware' and was used for many different useful household items. An example of this jug reported to be marked with a Charles Meigh lozenge is in a private collection. Unfortunately it is not available for viewing.

Height: 7¹/₄ inches
Unmarked
From the Morpeth Collection

40
Jousting Jug
William Ridgway, Son & Co
1 September 1840

This jug was probably designed to commemorate the Eglington Tournament of 1839. The mediaeval jousting figures are under a series of Gothic arches as in so many jugs of this period. Added decoration of freely twining grapevines surrounds the bottom of a blue stoneware body. Also found in light green and tan stoneware and in white parian.

Height: 11³/₄ inches
Impressed: Ridgway Mark
Published by
W. Ridgway, Son & Co.
Hanley
Sept. 1, 1840
4

41
'Stag'
Stephen Hughes c. 1842

The design of this blue stoneware jug is obviously copied from Ridgway's 'Jousting Jug', illustrated in No. 40. Stags both running and in respose replace the jousting figures of Ridgway. Two metal plugs indicate a lost lid but otherwise the design is identical. Of special interest are the metal staples which were driven into the jug to hold it together when it was broken. Stapling was a common practice in Victorian times and indicates that the owner valued his jug to have gone to so much trouble. This jug was also produced c. 1840 by Enoch and Edward Wood and was illustrated by Cork and Edge in their catalogue for the 1855 Paris Universal Exhibition.

Height: 8³/₄ inches
Impressed: **S. Hughes**

41a
'Stag' with Ceramic Lid
Stephen Hughes c. 1840

A few Victorian jugs originally had ceramic lids, however most of these have been broken over the years. Here we have a fine example of one that has survived. It is identical in design and colour to No. 41. This identical jug was produced circa 1840 by Enoch and Edward Wood, Burslem.

Height: 8³/₄ inches
Impressed: **S. Hughes**
From the Morpeth Collection

42
'Roman'
Charles Meigh 1 October 1840

This more sophisticated jug in tan smear-glazed stoneware is decorated with a formalized arrangement of acanthus leaves. There is a well-defined scalloped foot.

Height: 6¹/₂ inches
Impressed in cartouche:
Oct 1st
1840
Published by C. Meigh
Hanley
Roman
30
From the Morpeth Collection

43
Monkey Jug
Staffordshire Potteries c. 1840

This unmarked blue glazed earthenware jug is very similar in shape and design to other illustrated Staffordshire jugs (see illustrations Nos 32 and 36). It pictures a band of monkeys smoking and drinking and was produced by several different potters in earthenware, parian and stoneware. The theme is taken from David Tennier the Younger's painting *The Smoking Party* which hangs in the British Museum. The Latin Motto translates 'How much this ugly beast resembles us'. (*Apollo Magazine*, August 1981, p. 97.)

Height: 6¼ inches
Unmarked

44
'Good Samaritan'
Jones & Walley 1 November 1841

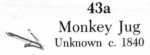

43a
Monkey Jug
Unknown c. 1840

A monkey scene identical to that found on jug No. 43, is here placed on a totally different shape of jug. The clay is tan stoneware.

Height: 8 inches
Unmarked

Another potter of particularly high quality moulded jugs was Jones and Walley who published their wares for only two years from 1841 to 1843. Here we have recalled the Biblical story of the Good Samaritan who rode by and stopped to help the more unfortunate man lying in the road. The jug is potted in light-green smear glaze stoneware.

Also found in tan.

Height: 8½ inches
Impressed:
Godden's Jones & Walley Mark No.
2224

Published Nov. 1, 1841
by Jones & Walley
Cobridge
Good Samaritan
12

Registered March 17, 1842
By Charles Meigh
Hanley
30
34

46
'Apostles' Modified
Charles Meigh 17 March 1842

45
'Apostles' Jug
Charles Meigh 17 March 1842

The 'Apostles' Jug by Charles Meigh is
one of the two or three best known and
most loved of the Victorian moulded
jugs. The straight sided angular octagonal shape was used to accommodate the
inevitable Gothic arches. It is produced
here in tan stoneware with a metal lid
to enhance its usefulness. Also found in
white.

Height: 7¼ inches
Impressed beneath Royal Arms:

A jug exactly as in illustration No. 45 except the religious figures set in Gothic arches have been replaced with Gothic type windows. It is reported that the Apostles were removed in order to appeal to Protestants who might object to having pictures of Saints in their homes. Also found in white.

Height: 9 inches
Mark as in No. 45 with the size number 12.

47
'Gipsey' (sic)
Jones & Walley 1 July 1842

The tan stoneware jug of oval shape depicts a group of gypsies camping and cooking in the woods, a particularly interesting jug both in shape and design. Also found in grey green.

Height: 6³/₄ inches
Impressed:

Published July 1, 1842
by
Jones & Walley
Cobridge
24 (size)
Gipsey (sic)

47a
'Gipsey' (sic)
Samuel Alcock & Co. 1 July 1842

Moulds for the various designs of jugs were passed from potter to potter or filched as the case may be. Sometimes designers took the moulds with them as they moved from factory to factory, thus many designs were reproduced exactly by several different factories. This 'Gipsey' Jug is a good case in point as it is identical to the Jones and Walley as described above in No. 47, except that it was made in lavender and white parian rather than tan stoneware. Also found in all-white parian.

Height: 4 inches
Impressed in cartouche:
> **Published by**
> **S. Alcock and Co.**
> **Burslem**
> **July 1st, 1842**

Note that the publishing date is identical with Jones and Walley.

48
Bacchanalian Dance
Charles Meigh 30 September 1844

Nicholas Poussin's painting *Bacchanalian Revels* hanging in the National Gallery inspired the design of this white stoneware jug. Grapevines and a Bacchic scene of many dancing figures abound over the surface in very deep relief. This is another popular and sought after Charles Meigh creation. Again, the reasonably straight sides of the jug provide a departure from the usual bulbous shape of the mid-1840s. Also found in tan.

Height: 9³/₄ inches
Impressed beneath Royal Arms:
> **Sept. 30, 1844**
> **Registd No. 21960**
> Registration Diamond
> **Sept. 30, 1844 Parcel 7**
> **Charles Meigh**
> **12** (size)

From the Morpeth Collection

48a
In 1847 the Society of Arts presented Charles Meigh with a medal for his mug using the same Bacchanalian design.

48b

Interesting mark on the bottom of No. 48a.

49
Nesting Birds
Mason's Patent Ironstone c. 1845

Here Masons used their ironstone body with an unusual greyish-tan overall glaze. The typical hexagonal shape has been drawn out to be wider than it is deep. Wandering tree branches hold

nesting birds in a design with strong Japanese influence. A snake forms the handle.

Height: 7½ inches
Printed: Godden's Mason's Crown Mark No. 2528
Printed: Mason's Patent Ironstone China

50
'Ranger'
Edward Walley, Cobridge
10 May 1845

A kneeling gamekeeper aiming his gun and flanked by two dogs are in sharp relief on one side of this grey-green stoneware jug, while a poacher leading his horse and followed by two dogs and another poacher covers the other. A scalloped foot and a tree branch handle complete the motif. Also found in tan. The registration number for this jug in the Design Patent Office is No. 27482. This identical design was registered under its number for both E. Walley and T. & R. Boote. Please note Illustration No. 50a.

Height: 7 inches
Impressed:
>Registration Diamond
>**24**
>Note: See Godden's E. Walley
>Mark No. 3988, plate 8.

Courtesy of Richard Riley Antiques

50a

The line drawing is taken from the Design Registration Books in the Public Records Office, Reference Code: Class 4, BT.43.64.

51
Stag and Hounds
Unknown c. 1845

Except for the handle, the shape of this white stoneware jug is identical to that of 'Ranger', No. 50, which was registered by Edward Walley and T. & R. Boote in 1845. One would like to attribute it to one of these fine potters. One side depicts a running stag chased by hounds. The reverse shows a standing stag with two does. The animals stand in an extensive and detailed landscape.

Height: 10 inches
Unmarked

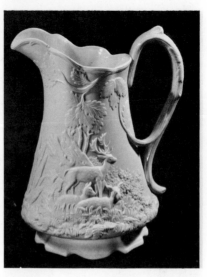

52
Dancing Amorini
Minton 20 March 1845

The little naked children of neuter sex illustrated on so many moulded jugs are called 'amorini' (derived from 'amor', to love) or 'putti', or sometimes 'cupids'. Here they are shown in deep relief on a white glazed stoneware jug holding hands as if in some game or dance. They are always shown in some form of play swinging from the top of the jug, shooting arrows, or playing with flowers.

Note the smaller foot rim, a forerunner of the 1850s when the definite foot gives way to the foot rim. Minton also issued this jug with the amorini changed to ivy leaves. The body for this jug was an experimental one produced for a short time by Minton. It was a substance between parian and stoneware.

Height: 9 inches
Impressed: Godden's Mark No. 2690, No. 228 (pattern)
Impressed: Registration Diamond

12B

53
Falstaff
Thomas Furnival & Co Miles Bank, Hanley December 30 1845

A very rare cane-coloured jug made by a company which was only in business from 1844 to 1846. The bigger-than-life body of Falstaff in deep relief sits in a chair holding his mug of beer. His head forms the neck and spout, his arm the handle. The body of the jug is tan stoneware.

Height: 7 inches
Embossed: Registration Diamond with **T. F. & Co.** incised in the border of the diamond

54
'Toho'*
Mason's Ironstone c. 1845

Four hunting dogs, moulded then applied stand out in very deep relief among the foliage and buildings of an English countryside. On either side around the neck of the jug sit two men drinking at a table surrounded by their dogs, guns and animals killed. They seem to be toasting their success. The body is of grey stoneware with a tree trunk handle. This jug bears the printed angular crown mark (c. 1845), however the shape and design is that of Mason jugs c. 1820–1830.

Height: 8½ inches
Printed: Godden's Mason's Angular Crown Mark, No. 2529
Impressed: **TOHO** inside an embossed cartouche

* Toho is a command to stop given to a hunting dog.

55
Boar and Stag Hunt
Mason's Ironstone c. 1845

This is a tan stoneware Mason's version of the kill with two dogs attacking a stag on one side, and with three dogs fighting a wild boar on the other. Tree branches twine in and out, ending in a tree trunk handle. As in jug No. 54, the Mason's angular crown mark on The Kill indicates a date of production c. 1845, though the

design is that of the 1820s.

56
'Portland Vase'
Samuel Alcock & Co. c. 1845

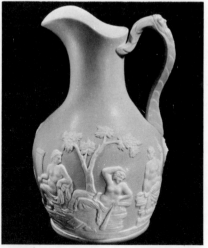

Perhaps the most important vase on record from classical times is the lovely first-century Portland Vase made of cameo glass. It came into the possession of the Duke of Portland in the eighteenth century and has been copied many times since. It was an inevitable source of design to the Victorians. This Alcock copy is in the form of a lavender and white parian jug with classical figures standing and in repose. After 1839 some copies of the vase show the figures partly clothed, as does this one, to comply with Victorian modesty. Wedgwood also produced this design both in black and white and in dark blue and white. Cork and Edge had a version which was in the 1855 Exhibition.

Height: 8 inches
Printed: **Patent**
           Samuel Alcock & Co.
           Godden's Mark No. 78

57
'Wisdom and Providence'
Possibly Samuel Alcock & Co. c. 1851

Two figures in Roman dress with rays emanating from their heads representing Wisdom and Providence form the design of the tan stoneware jug. Every inch of the surface is covered with symbols and figures. This is an excellent example of the Victorian emphasis on assorted

virtues. Also found in white. This design was introduced by Samuel Alcock, but it also was produced by David Crowe of Montrose.

Height: 6½ inches
Impressed: **24**
               L
Printed: **117**
From the Morpeth Collection

58
Battle of Acre
Samuel Alcock & Co. c. 1845

A commemorative jug immortalizing the Battle of Acre in 1799 when the British Navy assisted the people of Acre to resist the Napoleonic onslaught. The lavender background on which the white figures stand is a colour very typical of Samuel Alcock. This is one of the many jugs illustrated in this volume which were from a material developed in 1842 called parian. The far warmer appearance of the body obtained by parian made it more desirable for statuary and jugs than the cold white biscuit china body of the early nineteenth century. Who truly invented parian remains a mystery in

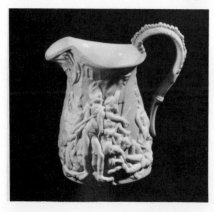

Alcock again uses their lovely lavender and white parian in a pattern almost identical to the Cork and Edge version of 'Babes in the Woods'.

Height: 6 inches
Printed: Godden's Alcock Mark No. 78
Printed: **143**

spite of claims by many factories and individuals to have done so. There has been some difference of opinion as to which battle this jug commemorates. According to the National Army Museum, it does depict the Battle of Acre and is taken from a print of that battle.

Height: 5 inches
Printed: Godden's Alcock Mark No. 78
Printed: **116**

59
'Babes in the Woods'
Samuel Alcock & Co. c. 1845

60
'Distin Family'
Samuel Alcock & Co. c. 1845

This jug commemorates the formation of the Distin Family Brass Band, which was the forerunner of this kind of band as we know it today. John Distin was born in 1798, played a slide trumpet in the South Devon Militia in the early 1800s, was married and had four sons: George, Henry, William and Theodore. In 1837 he formed a 5 instrument band with his four sons on brass instruments and his wife on the piano. The family went on to form a business making brass instruments and publishing music.

Lavender figures of Distin and his four sons surround the jug of white parian, a design also made by Cork and Edge.

Height: 9 inches
Printed: Godden's Alcock Mark No. 78
From the collection of Carl Pearson

61
Wedding at Gretna Green
Copeland & Garrett Late Spode
c. 1845

The motif for this jug comes from a painting by an unknown artist illustrated in James Ayres' account of England's distinctive folk art, *English Naive Painting including 1750 through 1900.* The sprigged scene shows the forge at Gretna Green where young couples in

Victorian times eloped to be married. On one side of the jug a couple arrive in a carriage at the smithy. On the reverse Shakespeare's Falstaff is bundled into a basket by the merry wives of Windsor. The design is on grey-green stoneware. Also found in white and in tan. It is interesting to note that this design is on a John Turner mould. In 1806 Turner went bankrupt, at which time Copeland bought and used many of the moulds designed and used by that firm.

Height: 7 inches
Impressed: Godden's Copeland & Garrett Mark No. 1092
Courtesy of Richard Riley Antiques

62
Youth and Old Age
Copeland & Garrett Late Spode
c. 1845

The contrast between youth and old age is represented here in a low tan stoneware jug. Youth is portrayed by three putti, leading and playing with a goat. Five satyrs in a drinking scene portray age, a fitting comment on the pleasures found in each time of life. This jug once

had a ceramic lid, which is now lost.

Height: 7 inches
Impressed: Godden's Copeland &
   Garrett Mark No. 1092
Impressed: **31**
Courtesy of Richard Riley Antiques

63
St Peter
Unknown c. 1845

Religious themes were commonly used
in the Victorian era to decorate various
household items. Here we have the Holy
Family on one side of the blue earthenware jug and St Peter denying Christ as
the cock crows thrice on the other. The
handle seems to be intended to
represent the serpent in the Garden of
Eden, though it is a very strange shaped
snake.

Height: 9 inches
Unmarked
From the Morpeth Collection

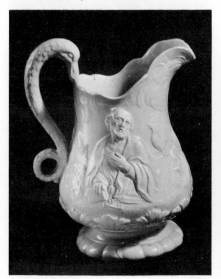

64
Foxes and Hounds
Minton c. 1831

This is a very interesting high relief jug
in pale grey-green stoneware which
depicts a group of four dogs on one side
and four foxes on the other. The handle
is in the form of a fox. Foliage completes
the ornate decoration of the jug. Because
the noses of the animals protrude a half

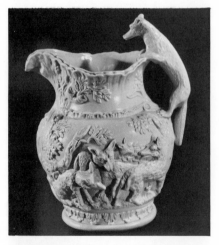

of an inch, it is almost impossible to find a jug on which at least one nose is not missing or replaced. The well defined fox handle is also very vulnerable.

Height: 8¹/₄ inches
Impressed: Godden's Minton Mark No. 2690
Impressed: **No 176**

From the Morpeth Collection

65
'Waverly Papers'
Minton c. 1835

Sir Walter Scott stands forth in very high relief on one side of this light green stoneware jug surrounded by the Scottish emblems, thistles and bagpipes. On the other side is a book open to chapter 12 of Scott's *Waverly Papers*.

Height: 9 inches
Impressed inside a cartouche:
 Godden's Mark No. 2960 **No. 919**
From the Morpeth Collection

66
Hunt Jug
Minton c. 1845

This is a jug very much in the style of the late eighteenth century Turner hunt jugs, however the Minton mark on the bottom of this jug is that used during the 1830s and 1840s by Minton (see Godden's Mark No. 2690). Thus it would seem that it must be dated much later than the early hunt patterns which it copies. The sprigged white stoneware body depicts the usual hunters, dogs, guns and foliage. A blue band surrounds the top through which runs an applied band of grape-vines.

Height: 6 inches
Embossed: Godden's Minton Mark No. 2690 with the pattern No. **225** impressed within.

67
Hanging Game
Unknown c. 1845

This style of jug with hanging dead game and dog handle was made in all types of pottery by many firms in virtually identical designs. This is of an unidentified potter in typical dark brown and tan glazed stoneware.

Height: 8 inches
Unmarked

got one very similar in blue, good condition.

67a
Hanging Game
William Shiller & Sons Germany
c. 1845

Compare this jug to No. 67. While the colour is different, the design is the same. The body, however, is earthenware covered with a reddish brown laquer and is called Siderolith ware and the jug a later German copy of an English design.

Height: 7¹/₂ inches
Impressed: **W. S. & S.**

Height: 5³/₄ inches
Impressed: **W. Ridgway, Son & Co.
Hanley**
Impressed: **24**

69
Fruits and Wheat
Herbert Minton & Co. 26 May 1846

This is a simply designed jug with fluting around the bottom and a band of white fruits and wheat in relief on a blue stippled background. The body is of creamy white parian, a medium that Minton, Copeland and Worcester developed to a fine art with many graceful and elegant designs. It is often difficult to distinguish between the work of these three potters, but as a generality, Minton parian is not as deep a cream as that of Copeland and it often has a more delicate look. The Society of Arts awarded Minton a prize for this jug.

68
Barrel
William Ridgway, Son & Co. c 1845

A light blue stoneware jug in the shape of a barrel with three strand stays. There is a high lip and an angular handle.

Height: 4¹/₂ inches
Embossed: Registration Diamond
   headed by a large ribbon impressed with
   Society of Arts Prize Jug 1846 and
   M. & Co.
Embossed: Godden's Minton Mark No.
   2690 with pattern No. **277** impressed

70
'Vintage'
Minton Patented: 26 May 1846
Produced: 1862

Here a wandering grape-vine pattern flows into the handle, which is in the shape of a grape-vine trunk. The white stoneware jug was the Society of Arts' prize jug for 1846. Starting in 1842, Minton impressed small cypher marks into the body usually in sets of three. These marks indicated the year of production, month of production, and potter's mark. Though patented in 1846, the jug carries the year cypher for 1862. See Godden's *Encyclopaedia of British Pottery and Porcelain Marks*, p. 440.

Height: 5 inches
Impressed: **Minton**
     E 306
Impressed: Year Cypher for 1862

Height: 3 inches
Embossed: Cartouche with **Copeland**
Impressed: **30**

71
Chinese Figures
Unknown c. 1846

Another Gothic arch jug, this time with rather incongruous Chinese figures standing within the arches. It is very similar to an 1846 T. J. & J. Mayer jug on which figures of Apostles replace the Chinese figures. A light jug made of blue glazed earthenware.

70a
Vintage
Copeland & Garrett c. 1846

Copeland produced the Vintage pattern in white parian, copying almost exactly the Minton jug, see No. 70.

[59]

Height: 5 inches
Unmarked

72
'Minster'
Charles Meigh 12 November 1846

Meigh has designed another white stoneware Gothic jug, this time with a beautifully moulded Madonna, Christ and St John the Baptist set in the arches. Gothic emblems surround the bottom. A very unusual handle has been added to make this a truly beautiful creation. Note the two little holes in the rim, these were put there to accommodate a metal lid, but do not necessarily mean the jug ever had one. Also found in tan.

Height: 8 inches
Impressed:

Nov 12, 1846 21
Registd 38068 49
Registration Diamond
Charles Meigh
Minster Jug

73
'Naomi'
Samuel Alcock & Co. 27 April 1847

If one had to choose the most sought-after moulded jug ever made, it probably would be this 'Minster'. Of the Victorian jugs, it is one of the most expensive.

Naomi and her two daughters-in-law are pictured on each side of this lavender and white parian jug with scalloped base.

Note how the dimensions of the jug have been changed from the norm and skilfully designed to meet the proportions and positioning of the figures, a design most similar to Arabic, No. 74. Biblical themes were common to this era. Also found in tan stoneware and white stoneware.

Height: 7³/₄ inches
Printed: Black Registration Diamond
Naomi and her daughters-in-law

early 1850s Charles Coxon copied this jug in the form of a tea-pot for the American firm of Edwin and William Bennett. They called it 'Rebecca at the Well' and produced it in enormous quantities for the American market. The inspiration for this design was Poussin's painting, *Rebecca at the Well.*

Height: 7¹/₄ inches
Printed: **Arabic** in black
Impressed: **30**
From the Morpeth Collection

74
'Arabic'
Samuel Alcock & Co. c. 1847

The shape and texture of 'Arabic' is almost identical to the Samuel Alcock jug 'Naomi' (illustration No. 73). A more slender graceful jug than some of its predecessors, its slim white stoneware body pictures a graceful Arabic woman – drawing water from a well. A scalloped foot adds to its beauty. There is a marked example in the City Museum in Stoke on Trent, Alcock Pattern No. 186. In the

75
'Hop Jug'
Herbert Minton & Co. 14 May 1847

Mr Henry Cole commissioned Mr Henry J. Townsend to design this 'Hop Jug' for his Summerly's Art Manufacturer. Mintons registered the design on 14 May 1847 and produced it in stoneware with coloured glazes and in creamy white parian. It is heavily decorated with cherubs, nude figures, Victorian figures and many hop vines covering the entire surface. There is a metal lid with a cherub and two sheafs of wheat as a finial.

Height: 8¼ inches
Embossed: Godden's Minton Mark No. 2690 with **No. 320** inside ribbon
Embossed: Registration Diamond
Courtesy of Don and Elizabeth Davis

76
Bullrushes
Ridgway & Abington 7 March 1848

In the last half of the 1840s, another dramatic change took place in which the entire appearance of jugs was altered. The prominent foot became a narrow foot-rim, the body weight started to rise, relief was usually more shallow, and a naturalistic arrangement of plant life replaced the figures and animals of earlier times. At the Paris Exhibition of 1844 *Art Union Magazine* used the term 'running patterns' to describe the new design. All the potteries started to produce jugs in keeping with the new look. Even jugs which subsequently used animals and figures would be found to include these 'running patterns' of plant life in the design. Bullrushes illustrates perfectly this new naturalistic trend. It is potted in tan stoneware.

Height: 6 inches and 5 inches
Impressed: Registration Diamond
From the Morpeth Collection

77
Hops and Barley
Ridgway & Abington 7 March 1848

In Hops and Barley, we have the new shape of jug, but the design goes back to a more formal look. Elizabethan strapwork divides the jug into six panels containing hops and barley in a repeating pattern. The angular handle also recalls Tudor times in this heavy tan stoneware example. Also found in white.

Height: 8¾ inches
Impressed: Registration Diamond
Impressed: **12**

78
'Trellis Jug'
Charles Meigh 18 September 1848

An especially fine quality white parian jug covered with a trellis and vines. The body weight is very low, making it most graceful.

Height: 5 inches
Embossed: Tree branch in a circle
Impressed: Inside a circle:

Trellis Jug
Registered
Sept. 18, 1848
No. 54487

Embossed and Impressed in centre of circle: Registration Diamond

79
Infant Samuel
T. & R. Boote 17 October 1848

In 1847, T. & R. Boote of Burslem ushered in a new era with the introduction of a basically straight sided jug which had only a slight taper at the top. This was the forerunner of the tankard shape, variations of which were used by Boote and other firms intermittently until the late 1870s. At this time the true tankard came on to the scene and has remained the most popular design for household jugs ever developed. On this tan stoneware body we have the 1847

Boote shape with a cut-away foot rim and a spout which is upward flaring. Another religious subject, it depicts the Infant Samuel telling Eli of his vision under a Gothic arch in the Temple. Also found in white.

Height: 9 inches
Printed: Registration Diamond

80
Bouquet
Probably H. & R. Daniels c. 1848

Three bouquets of assorted flowers in blue relief surround this stoneware jug of grey colour. There is a angular handle which is a departure from the usual curved or stylized ones of this period. Blue bead work surrounds a small foot. On the bottom is a blue embossed mark incorporating two small angels holding a flower type of swag enclosing an incised No. 74. To date this mark is unidentified. Also found in porcelain.

[63]

Height: 8 inches
Unidentified mark
Courtesy of Richard Riley Antiques

81
'Sylvan'
Ridgway & Abington
16 February 1849

A grey-green stoneware jug with lid on which ivy grows freely on vertical bamboo canes. This is one of the last jugs to use the distinct pedestal foot instead of a small foot ring. It has also been found in white.

Height: 6½ inches
Impressed: Registration Diamond

80a
Unidentified mark on bottom of Bouquet jug No. 80. Probably H. & R. Daniels.

82
Lily of the Valley
W.T. Copeland 9 November 1849

This particularly lovely white parian jug depicts single stalks of lily of the valley randomly placed over large leaves.

Height: 8¼ inches
Impressed: **COPELAND** plus
Registration Diamond

a prize-winning jug in the 1851 Exhibition, made of blue and white parian. Also found in all white parian.

Height: 9 inches
Printed: Company Crest, Godden's
Mark No. 2571, with **Prize Medal 1851** above Crest. Also printed Regi-

83
Birdnesting
T. J. & J. Mayer Dale Hall
Pottery Longport 2 July 1850

Again we have a tree stump jug, very similar to the 'Convolvulus' pattern (see No. 84). A naughty little boy climbs among the wandering tree branches trying to reach a bird's nest containing eggs. On the reverse side we find him successful. The deep relief used on this jug recalls the previous decade. This was

stration (83 contd) Diamond and an embossed ribbon with No. **29** and No. **12** incised.

84
'Convolvulus' Jug
T. J. & J. Mayer 19 December 1850

In order to stress a naturalistic appearance, many jugs were designed in the form of tree stumps with various bits of foliage growing around or climbing on them. The lovely Mayer blue and white parian 'Convolvulus' design is one such. This pattern was pictured in the *Art Journal Catalogue* of the Great 1851 Exhibition. Also found in all white parian.

Height: 7 inches
Impressed: Registration Diamond with **47** within a ribbon

85
'Death of Sir Robert Peel'
T. & R. Boote c. 1850

The death of Sir Robert Peel (29 July 1850) is commemorated on a grey-green stoneware jug. The figure of Sir Robert stands on each side in white relief. There is white scroll work at the top, a white band at the bottom, and a bamboo handle. On the under side of the jug is printed the following poem:

> Farewell great statesman!
> Long will thy honest worth be miss'd
> In the councils of the nation.
> And when the time of England's difficulty comes
> Then will the people truly feel
> The Patriot they have lost.

A picture of a lamenting female at a tombstone heads the poem.

Height: 6½ inches
Printed: **Patent Mosaic T. & R. Boote**
From private collection

86
Camel
Samuel Alcock & Co. c. 1850

This is an early tankard-style jug with high handle and scalloped rim made from grey stoneware. On each side of the jug there is a man leading a camel and rider set among many tropical palm trees. The rider carries a prominent gun which may indicate that the camel train has come across a dangerous desert.

Height: 7½ inches
Impressed: **21** and small **o**

87
'Ariadne'
Samuel Alcock & Co. c. 1850

This lovely lavender and white jug, a colour typical of Samuel Alcock, is decorated with the graceful nude figure of Ariadne of Greek mythology, daughter of Minos, King of Crete. Ariadne fell in love with Theseus when he came to Crete to slay the Minotaur and gave him

a thread to guide him through the labyrinth. Theseus slew the Minotaur, carried off Ariadne, then abandoned her on Naxos.

Here on the parian jug she reclines on a drapery half covering a large lioness. The only other decoration consists of grape-vines which form a handle and surround the neck of the jug.

A very interesting feature of the jug is the treatment on the reverse. The same

figure of Ariadne reclines on the lioness, except that it is shown as it would look from behind.

Height: 9 inches
Printed: Godden's Alcock Mark No. 78
From the collection of Carl Pearson

88
Flowers and Barley
Samuel Alcock & co. c. 1850

The two large knops in the middle of the long neck make the shape of this jug most unusual. A few white flowers are interspersed among white stalks of barley on a lavender parian body. An undulating stalk of barley forms the handle.

Height: 10 inches
Printed: Godden's Alcock Mark No. 78
Printed: **195**

89
Cain and Abel
Samuel Alcock & co. c. 1850

This lovely lavender and white parian jug depicts another Biblical scene, this time the story of Cain and Abel. On one side in crisp white relief is Cain as he kills his brother. On the other side, the grief-stricken Mother and Father find their slain son. A white leaf forms the

handle on the stippled lavender background. This design was first registered on 3 June 1854 by Thomas Till and Co., not by Alcock.

Height: 10 inches
Printed: Godden's Alcock Mark No. 78
Printed: **252**

90
'Aristo'
Samuel Alcock & co. c. 1850

Another Alcock lavender and white parian jug. The white busts of Aristo and Tasso are in twin circles. Ivy vines cover

the bowl, the spout is a mask and there are masks at each end of the angular handle.

Height: 7¼ inches
Printed: Godden's Alcock Mark No. 78

91
Bullrushes
Unknown c. 1850

A small white parian jug decorated with naturalistic bullrushes around the bowl.

Height: 4½ inches
Unmarked

92
Toby Filpot with Bacchus Head
Unknown c. 1850

The potter worked his sense of humour overtime when he designed this white parian jug. He used the body of Toby Filpot for the bowl of the jug, but he placed a Bacchus head on top for the neck and spout.

Height: 4½ inches
Unmarked

Height: 4½ inches
Unmarked

93
Victorian Girl
Unknown c. 1850

Another white parian jug on which a
figure is used for the bowl, neck and
spout. The full figure of a girl in a lovely
hooped skirted dress and a muff forms
the bowl. Her hat is the spout.

94
Two Drivers
(AKA: Coach and Railway)
Minton c. 1850

This is a very important Minton jug
commemorating the advent of the train,
an innovation which drastically changed
the life of all Victorians. It is designed in
unglazed terracotta-coloured stoneware
on the outside and dark brown glaze on

the inside. Two medallions contain the two drivers, the coaching driver and the railway engineer. The coaching scene bears the date 1800 and includes an inn, 'The Traveller's Rest'. The train scene shows an engine passing under a bridge with the date 1848. This jug was designed by Henry J. Townsend and made by Minton, originally for Henry Cole's Summerly's Art Manufacturers. Mr Cole was instrumental in organizing the 1851 Exhibition and in the conception of the Victoria and Albert Museum. His Summerly's Art Manufacturers scheme was an effort to involve important artists in the creation of decorative arts. Though designed in the middle of the century, the Minton date code indicates that this specific jug was produced in 1870.

Height: 8¼ inches
Impressed: Minton M 336 6

95
Resting Putti
Unknown c. 1850

This white parian jug is very well moulded considering its tiny size. On each side reclines a putto in a spray of vegetation set on a stippled background. Rococo style curves decorate the rim.

Height: 3 inches
Unmarked

96
Storks Among the Grapes
Unknown c. 1850

Two storks stand among many freely growing grape-vines on a white parian jug.

Height: 7½ inches
Unmarked

97
Grapes, Flowers & Grain
Unknown c. 1850

The fine quality of this white parian body would probably indicate manufacture by Minton or Copeland. A twining grape-vine forms the handle which continues into the body of the jug intertwined with wheat stalks, grape leaves and fruit.

Height: 8½ inches
Unmarked

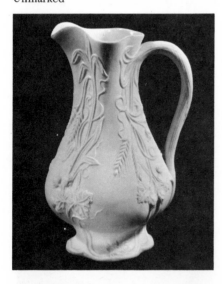

98
Swans
Probably Ridgway & Abington c. 1850

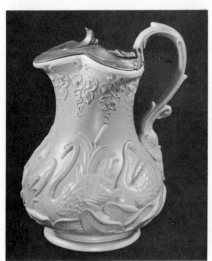

A scalloped neck tan stoneware jug featuring swans floating among naturalistic bullrushes. The finial of the handle is a swan in repose. This design was produced by both Ridgway & Abington and by Robert Heron of Scotland.

Height: 8 inches
Unmarked
From the Morpeth Collection

99
'The Jolly Toper'
W. T. Copeland c. 1845

On one side of a tan stoneware jug a portly gentleman sits at a barrel (in a pub, perhaps?) smoking his pipe, with his drink on the barrel. On the other side his more rotund friend sits at a table holding his foaming mug of beer and his pipe. Both scenes are surrounded by grapes, vines, and other plants. The handle is the typical branch of a tree.

Height: 7 inches
Impressed: **Copeland**
Impressed: **12**

very similar to this in heavily glazed tan stoneware, the sketch for which was done by Lady Diana Beauclerk, whose sketches and drawings were used by Wedgwood for their cameos and bas-reliefs.

Height: 6½ inches
Impressed: **Copeland** in cartouche
Impressed: **19**

100
'The Vintage'
W. T. Copeland c. 1845

101
Music and the Dance
Unknown c. 1850

This is a white parian jug covered with eight putti harvesting grapes, making wine, and drinking the finished product. There is a twisted tree branch handle. Copeland produced this design in 8 different sizes which sold at the time for from three to ten shillings. In 1870 Wedgwood designed and potted a jug

On one side of a blue and white stippled parian jug two mediaeval figures dance while a seated boy plays a stringed instrument. On the reverse a lad plays a flute while a child reclines against an attentive girl clutching a pillow. The scenes are set among flowers and foliage. The shade of cream parian plus the lovely quality could indicate a Copeland origin.

Height: 8 inches
Unmarked

is parian.

Height: 6 inches
Unmarked

103
'Nymphea'
W. T. Copeland 30 May 1851

A parian jug with large waterlilies and pods in relief. It is all white.

102
Putti and Grapes
Unknown c. 1850

A similar theme to jug No. 100. Here the putti sit holding grapes and kneeling and drinking wine from a huge urn. An unusual pink stippled ground was used with white figures and grapes. The body

Height: 6 inches
Impressed inside cartouche:
Copeland 30
Impressed: Registration Diamond

104
'Nineveh'
Ridgway & Abington 16 August 1851

Assyrian archaeological findings by A. H.
Layard inspired the design of this
unusually shaped, white stoneware jug.
Twined snakes form a handle attached to
a neck surrounded by Assyrian letters.
A large winged bull with human head
stands on one side, a winged lion on the
reverse. Assyrian motifs are on the lower
half.

Height: 8½ inches
Impressed: A small heart
Impressed: Diamond Registration
Courtesy of Richard Riley Antiques

105
'Willie'
William Ridgway & Co. 21 October
1851

Willie, of the Robert Burns' poem of the
same name, sits drinking with two
friends on either side of this white stoneware jug. There is a twisted rope handle,
a pinched-in spout, and a band of leaves
on the neck.

Height: 5½ inches
Impressed: **WILLIE**
          W. R. & Co.
             2
          30 (size)

106
Thistle
Charles Meigh & Son 13 November
1851

This tan stoneware jug bears a large
thistle plant, freely growing, covering
the entire body of the jug. There is a
scalloped foot.

Height: 10¼ inches
Impressed: Registration Diamond
From the collection of Carl Pearson

81518

French novel by Bernardin de Saint Pierre. See jug No. 148 for another version of this theme.

Height: 8³/₄ inches
Impressed: **No. 102**
24
D 102

* There is some dispute as to the subject matter of the design of this jug. It is, however, commonly believed to be Paul et Virginie.

Photograph courtesy Public Record Office

108
Dancers
George Ray of Longton 21 April 1852

A flow blue underglaze has been applied to an earthenware body. The dancing couple seem to be dressed for a costume ball, their clothes painted in bright colours. The tankard shape and copper lustre trim all combine to make this moulded jug unusual for the period.

Height: 6 inches
Impressed: Registration Diamond

107
Paul et Virginie*
T. J. & J. Mayer 2 December 1851

This blue and white parian tankard-type jug illustrates the story of Paul and Virginie, the ill-fated lovers of the

109
Bacchanalian Cherubs
J. & T. Lockett 21 June 1852

Several amorini are playing 'Tug of War' under drooping fuchsia blossoms on a tan stoneware jug. Also found in blue and white parian.

Height: 6 inches
Impressed: Registration Diamond
From the Morpeth Collection

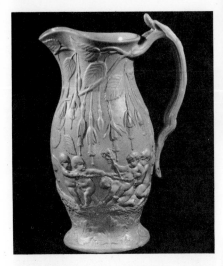

ware. Also found in all white and in a three piece drabware tea-set.

Height: 7 inches
Impressed: Registration Diamond

111
Six Virtues
Charles Meigh & Son c. 1852

110
Four Seasons
Charles Meigh & Son 25 August 1852

Charles Meigh & Son was a successor to the early Charles Meigh works from which so many beautiful jugs were designed in the 1830s and early 1840s. This jug has a crisply moulded mask spout and represents the four seasons of the year. In each of the four panels a cupid plays in a natural setting, typical of the season it represents. It is a very striking jug in dark blue and white stone-

This is another Meigh & Son, highly reminiscent of illustration No. 110, The Four Seasons. Here we have six classically dressed women in panels representing Faith, Justice, Hope, Temperance, Fortitude and Prudence, all favourite female virtues of the Victorians. The metal lid, which adds beauty and usefulness, has an interesting metal weight attached underneath which allows the top to fall back in place readily when released, an unusual feature. Made of blue and white stoneware. also found in glazed porcelain.

Height: 9 inches
Impressed in cartouche: **C. Meigh & Son Hanley**

112
Slavery
Ridgway & Abington 1 January 1853

In addition to producing millions of jugs for the English market, many of the potters made large numbers of jugs expressly for export to the United States. Here a theme has been taken from the book *Uncle Tom's Cabin* written by Harriet Beecher Stowe in 1852, denouncing the unhappy practice of slavery. Uncle Tom is seen on the auction block surrounded by figures of the auctioneer and bidders. A sign reads 'By auction this day, a prime lot of healthy negroes.' On the other side of the white stoneware jug is Little Eva being carried away by the angels while she is chased by Simon Legree. A real heart tugger. Also found in grey-green stoneware.

Height: 6¼ inches
Impressed: **Published by
E. Ridgway & Abington
Hanley
January 1, 1853**

From the Morpeth Collection

113
Snake and Dog
Parkhurst & Dimmock 22 June 1853

This large tankard-type white stoneware jug depicts the loyalty of a dog to his small boy master, as the dog attacks a snake near the reclining boy.

Surrounding the scene are naturalistic flowers, but the handle is in the shape of a stylized snake.

Height: 9³/₄ inches
Impressed: Registration Diamond
Impressed: **6**

1)

114
'Robinson Crusoe'
Stephen Hughes & Co. c. 1853

Here we have the children's story of the shipwreck of Robinson Crusoe. However, the hero is placed in a naturalistic setting of vegetation in keeping with the 1850s. A ram's head mask spout adds slightly incongruous interest to this grey stoneware jug.

Height: 6¹/₂ inches
Impressed: **S. Hughes & Co.**

115
Ivy Leaf
Samuel Alcock & Co. 30 January 1854

A pinched-lip tan stoneware version of the naturalistic design with ivy leaves and vines.

Height: 5³/₄ inches
Impressed: Registration Diamond
Impressed: **30**
Printed: Godden's Alcock Mark No. 78
From the Morpeth Collection

116
Horizonal Grape-vine
Samuel Alcock & Co. c. 1854

This small Alcock jug is made of white

parian, has a high handle and a scalloped rim. A prominent horizontal grape-vine encircles the bulbous body, and grape leaves cover the surface.

Height: 4 inches
Printed: Godden's Alcock Mark No. 78

A very understated design of scallops and swags surround a tan stoneware body. Two flowers join each end of the vine handle to the jug. This jug bears the early Ridgway anchor mark, although the design would indicate a later date.

Height: 7¹/₂ inches
Embossed: Godden's Ridgway & Co.
   Anchor Mark No. 3266
Courtesy of Richard Riley Antiques

118
'Hop Jug'
W. T. Copeland 12 September 1854

This is the Copeland version of the tankard, Wandering Plant Pattern jug of the 1850s. This time the background simulates barrel stays covered with hop vines. It is made of white stoneware.

Height: 6 inches
Impressed: Registration Diamond
Impressed: **30**

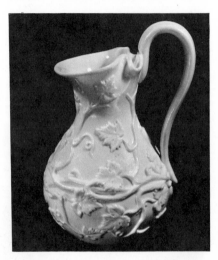

117
Simplicity
William Ridgway & Co. c. 1854

119
Grinning Bacchus
Unknown c. 1855

A broadly grinning face of Bacchus peers out of a background of grapes and vines on either side of a white parian jug.

Height: 5½ inches
Unmarked

120
The Wedding
Ridgway & Abington 1 January 1855

It would seem that Ridgway & Abington have copied the wedding scene used on the earlier Minton Wedding jug (see No. 35). Only the wedding figures are the same for, as you can see, the straight-sided shape of this jug, as well as the ornate decoration, differs drastically from the Minton product. The medium is grey stoneware.

Height: 9¾ inches
Impressed: Godden's Ridgway & Abington Mark No. 3249
From the collection of Carl Pearson

121
Three Soldiers
Ridgway & Abington
1 August 1855 (Indistinct)

On the Russian double eagle stand three soldiers, one English, one Scottish, one Turkish. They symbolize the allies of the Crimean War (1853–6), Britain, France, Sardinia and the Ottoman Empire, who fought and defeated Russia. The body of this jug is grey-green stoneware, the neck is scalloped and surrounded by beading which also goes down the angular handle.

Height: 9³/₄ inches
Impressed in an embossed cartouche:
**Published by E. Ridgway & Abington
Hanley
August 1, 1855** (Indistinct)
From a Private collection

122
Pineapple
James Dudson 6 August 1855

The James Dudson Company, today called Dudson Brothers, is most unusual in that it has remained in the hands of the Dudson family for eight generations. This firm produced great quantities of stoneware jugs during the Victorian era, the early ones being primarily thrown and sprigged, while the later ones were often relief moulded. This grey example has a pineapple motif.

Height: 9 inches
Impressed: **Dudson**
Impressed: Registration Diamond

123
Angel and Amorini
Worcester Kerr and Binns
Period c. 1855

Worcester made many beautiful white parian items of fine quality. However, very few marked examples are to be found. As always from this fine potter, the quality of the jug is exceptional. It is designed in a very bulbous shape with four panels on a stippled body. In two panels are freely wandering grape-vines, in two others are angels holding amorini.

Height: 7 inches
Printed: Standard blue Worcester mark
with four intertwining **Ws** in a circle

124
Grapevine
Worcester Kerr and Binns
Period c. 1855

A single grape-vine encircles the top of
this white parian jug, ending in a vine
trunk handle. The very bulbous bowl of
the jug has fluting broken by a line band.
Height: 5½ inches
Printed: Blue Worcester mark,
Godden's No. 4345, containing
pattern No. 31

126
'Vintage'
J. & M. P. Bell & Co. c. 1855

A white stoneware jug with amorini, this
time gathering grapes in the woods.

Height: 8¼ inches
Impressed in a semi-circle: **J. & M. P.
Bell & Co.**

125
'Cup Tosser' or Reading the
Tea Leaves
Worthington & Green c. 1855

A white glazed parian jug depicting a
gypsy telling the fortune of a young girl
from the tea leaves in the bottom of the
cup. This same theme was potted by
Cork and Edge and in 1855 was illustrated in the catalogue of the Paris
Exhibition.

Height: 8½ inches
Impressed: **Worthington & Green**

127
'Corn Husk'
J. & E. Norton Bennington,
Vermont, USA c. 1855,

This jug was produced by one of the Bennington companies in Vermont, USA. Mr Richard Carter Barret, in his book *Bennington Pottery and Porcelain*, tells us that it is one of the few jugs made by this firm which were not directly copied from English designs. The body is parian with white corn cobs and stalks on a blue stippled ground. The handle is formed by a stalk of corn.

Height: 6 inches
Unmarked

This jug was exhibited in the Paris Exhibition of 1855 by Cork & Edge.

Height: 8 inches
Unmarked

128
'Ino'
Probably Cork & Edge c. 1855

A large cherub stands among a heavy laden grape-vine on one side of this tan stippled stoneware jug. On the reverse sits a cherub reaching for the grapes.

129
'Babes In The Woods'
Probably Cork & Edge c. 1855

The children's pantomime *Babes In The Wood* inspired this glazed earthenware jug. The figures of the two children who are lost in the forest plus the foliage are highlighted with bright blue, red, yellow and green enamels over the glaze.

Height: 8¹/₄ inches
Unmarked

130
Musical Instruments
W. T. Copeland c. 1855

A mask of the Muse of Music under the spout is flanked by two Baroque cartouches containing all kinds of musical instruments. Light-blue smear glazed stoneware was used for the body. A jug obviously aimed at the musically inclined.

Height: 9³/₄ inches
Impressed: **Copeland**
                    9

131
'Swiss'
William Brownfield c. 1855

This is the first of the Brownfield jugs to be illustrated. William Brownfield, an excellent potter, produced prolific numbers of jugs made in basically identical shapes. At least 21 Brownfield patterns were registered between 1851 and 1883. Here he used a goat's head mask spout on a barrel stay body, a simply but effectively designed blue and white stoneware jug with lid.

Height: 7³/₄ inches
Impressed in a semi-circle band:

Swiss Impressed inside a Staffordshire
knot: 24
                    WB

WG

132
George Washington
Edward Walley 18 April 1856

Here is another of those moulded jugs
made in England for the American
market (see Slavery, Illustration No.
112), this one a tribute to George Washington, the Commanding General of the
American Revolutionary War and first
President of the United States. There is
a full-length image of Washington
holding his sword in one hand, a banner
saying 'American Independence' in the
other. On the reverse there is Washington with an old lady, perhaps Mrs
Washington. Draped flags of the 13
colonies separate the two groups of
figures. The jug was made of white
parian with an angular handle and metal
lid.

Height: 7 inches
Unmarked

133
'John Barleycorn'
Ridgway & Abington 18 April 1856

A free 'running plant' designed white
stoneware jug with stalks of barley
superimposed on criss-cross bands. Also
found in celadon green.

Height: 7½ inches
Impressed: Registration Diamond
Impressed: 3

134
Gothic Ivy
William Brownfield Cobridge
30 April 1856

Gothic arches with wandering ivy leaves
and berries form the body of this slim
white stoneware jug.

Height: 9 inches
Impressed: Registration Diamond
Courtesy of Richard Riley Antiques

This is a lovely, tall, blue and white stoneware jug with the graceful Amphitrite on each side surrounded by tritons riding on their dolphins. Amphitrite was goddess of the sea and married to the god Poseidon in Greek mythology. Produced in both parian and stoneware, the jug gives an aura of the much later art deco period. Also found in all white.

Height: 8 inches
Impressed: Registration Diamond
Impressed: **C. Meigh and Son**
Incised: **24**
Impressed: **16**

135
Amphitrite
Charles Meigh & Son 13 June 1856

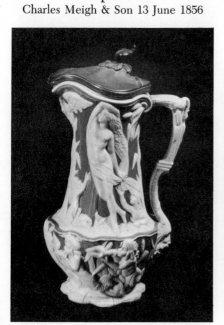

136
Fuchsia
Ridgway & Abington 14 October 1857

A white stoneware stippled jug covered by free running fuchsia plants.

Height: 8¼ inches
Impressed: Registration Diamond

[87]

137
'Gleaner'
Edward Walley, Cobridge
11 November 1858

On the reverse there is a man harvesting wheat. A large sheaf of wheat trails up the front of the jug and from the end of the handle on to a quilted background. The jug is of tan stoneware. The illustration is taken from the Public Records Office Design Registration Book, Reference Code: Class 4, BT.43.67.

Height: 10³/₄ inches
Impressed: **E. Walley**
      Cobridge
      November 11, 1858
From the collection of Carl Pearson

138
'Fern'
William Brownfield 5 November 1859

White fern fronds grow vertically up the white glazed stoneware body of the typically shaped Brownfield jug. Wheat hangs from the top. A Staffordshire knot has been added to a candy striped handle, and gilt applied for highlight.

Height: 8¹/₂, 7¹/₂ and 6¹/₂ inches
Impressed: Registration Diamond
      encircled by a band which reads:
      Fern 24 W. B. Cobridge

Here in fine relief and exquisite detail a girl stands in a wheat field carrying her gleaning tool, followed by a little lamb.

139
Diamond Checkerboard
Edward & William Walley 14
December 1859

A blue background carries a geometric pattern in white relief of diamonds diminishing in size toward the top of the jug. The stoneware body is decorated at the seams with large upright white leaves.

Height: 7¹/₂ inches
Unmarked

140
Scrolls and Flowers
William Brownfield 6 June 1860

The 1860s saw a new type of design develop which was formal and stylized rather than naturalistic. Flowers were still used but were in conjunction with scrolls and geometrics. This glazed stoneware jug is a typical 1860s creation with scrolls and stylized flowers in green, highlighted with gilt. Its metal lid adds both value and practicability. The shape is typically Brownfield.

Height: 10 inches
Impressed: Registration Diamond
12
Impressed inside Staffordshire
Knot:**WB**

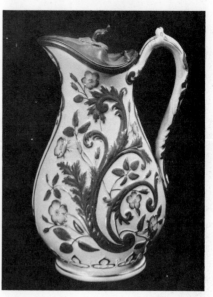

141
'The Loyal Volunteers'
Sanford Pottery 28 September 1860

Here is one of the commemorative jugs so popular today, this one recalling Queen Victoria's review of the Loyal Volunteers in London and Edinburgh. There is a bust of Queen Victoria dividing four standing military figures. The inscriptions reads 'Our Army and Navy and Brave Volunteers' and 'Defenders of our Queen and Country'. This very tall, slim, straight-sided jug is of white glazed stoneware.

Height: 10¹/₂ inches
Impressed: Registration Diamond
Impressed Inside ribbon:
Sanford Pottery
From the Morpeth Collection

142
Pine Cone
Bates & Co. 12 December 1860

During the 1860s, several designs of jugs were potted in which the leaves or fruit of the plants formed the entire jug, such as a pineapple jug by Minton (see illustration No. 184) and this pine cone jug by Bates & Co. The stoneware pine cone is white with a handle in the form of a limb of the pine tree.

Height: 5 inches
Impressed: Registration Diamond
Impressed: **36**
From the Morpeth Collection

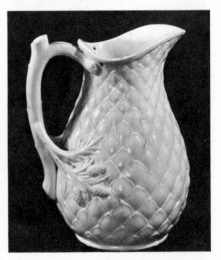

143
Stylized Vine
Unknown c. 1860

On each side of this tan stoneware jug are stylized vines and berries in crisp relief.

Height: 8 inches and 7 inches

Incised: **12**
Incised: **J**
From the Morpeth Collection

144
Sleeping Beauty
Unknown c. 1860

Here the wicked fairy disguised as an old
lady encourages the beautiful princess of
the fairy tale *Sleeping Beauty* to use the
poisoned spindle which will put her to
sleep for 100 years. The scene is
moulded in shallow relief on a blue
earthenware body.

Height: 7 inches
Unmarked

145
Wheatsheaf
James Dudson c. 1860

This white stoneware jug displays a large
sheaf of wheat surrounded by flowers.

Height: 9 inches
Unmarked

146
Chrysanthemum
Ridgway & Co. c. 1860

Scrolling vines and buds form a background for blue and white chrysanthemum blossoms which stand out in
deep relief on a green glazed stoneware
body. This jug has also appeared in all
light green and all white.

Height: 9¹/₄ inches
Impressed: **Published by Ridgway &
Co. England July 1, 1835**
It would seem that an earlier mark was
used on this jug of the 1860s.

Height: 4¹/₂ inches
Unmarked

148
'Paul et Virginie'
Unknown c. 1860

147
Grapes with Fluting
Unknown c. 1860

A white stoneware jug with metal lid. Grape vines wander around the stippled bowl, and fluting surrounds the neck and base.

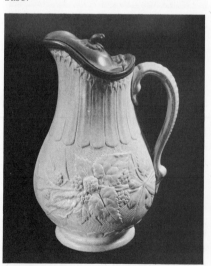

This grey stoneware octagonal shaped jug tells the operatic story of Paul and Virginie, two young star-crossed lovers. Set in eighteenth-century Africa, the young couple are separated by Virginie's Mother, Margaret, when the girl is sent back to France. Her ship is wrecked and her body washed ashore to be found by the disconsolate Paul. The French opera was written by Masson from a novel by Bernardin de Saint Pierre.

Height: 8 inches
Unmarked

149
Water Lilies
Unknown c. 1860

Another parian water lilies design (see illustration No. 103), this time in blue and white and unmarked.

Height: 8 inches
Unmarked

150
'New Pineapple'
James Dudson c. 1860

An all-over design of pineapple and grapes cover this green and white stoneware jug with a metal lid.

Height: 9½ inches
Impressed: **2/100**
Impressed: **0**
Courtesy of Richard Riley Antiques

151
Lily of the Valley
Unknown c. 1860

Lily of the Valley leaves and stalks of flowers encase the bottom of a light-grey stoneware jug with stippling on the body.

Height: 8 inches
Unmarked
Courtesy of Richard Riley Antiques

Height: 7 inches
Impressed: **N**

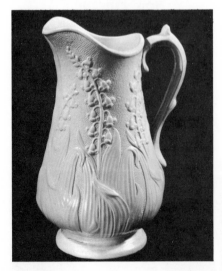

153
Freesia
Unknown c. 1860

The blue body of this stoneware jug is covered by upright canes. Two sprays of freesia on a long stem form the handle.

Height: 5 inches
Unmarked

152
Cattails and Flowers
Unknown c. 1860

154
'Shakespeare'
Unknown c. 1860

Shakespeare stands on one side of this little white parian jug, his bust with laurel leaves occupies the other. The relief is highlighted with various overglaze colours.

Another dark blue stoneware jug on which plants form the entire body, this time cattails and leaves. A vertical spray of flowers decorates each side.

Height: 3¹/₂ inches
Unmarked

156
Six Flowers
Unknown c. 1860

A white parian jug on which six flowers are placed in six eight-sided panels. Vertical leaves alternate with cattails around the bottom.

Height: 5 inches
Unmarked

155
'Dickens'
Unknown c. 1860

This white earthenware jug is glazed inside and out, a feature unusual for the period. On each side is a bust of Charles Dickens with a book above his head, open at the word 'Pickwick'. The body is heavily stippled and bright overglaze colours have been used as trim.

Height: 7½ inches
Unmarked

157
Basketweave
Cork Edge & Malkin 31 May 1861

A floral 'running pattern' on a blue ground with a basketweave bottom adorns this stoneware jug designed in the style of the 1850s.

Height: 8 inches
Printed; Godden's Cork Edge & Malkin Mark No. 1102
Impressed: Registration Diamond

Embossed: Ribbon swag with **Wedg-wood and Co** (not Josiah Wedgwood)
Painted: **1055**
Courtesy of Richard Riley Antiques

159
'Union'
William Brownfield 4 December 1861

Pottery was sometimes used to expound a cause (see illustration No. 112 Slavery). With this jug the maker was opting for union between England, Wales, Scotland and Ireland. In the stylized flora of the white stoneware jug we find the rose of England, the shamrock of Ireland, the thistle of Scotland and the feathers of Wales, thus the design is called 'Union'.

Height: 7³/₄ inches
Impressed: **Union**
Impressed: Registration Diamond
Impressed inside a Staffordshire Knot:
¹/₈ M W.B. 24

158
Stylized Blossoms
Wedgwood and Co. 22 August 1861

The bulbous stoneware body of this jug is covered with a bright lavender ground with white stylized flowers highlighted in gold. A metal lid was used.

Height: 7 inches
Impressed: Registration Diamond

160
'Harvey'
J. Dimmock & Co. c. 1862

A simply designed jug with a single long-stemmed snowdrop blossom on either side. Khaki-coloured stoneware was used for the body – an unusual colour. Mr Richard Carter Barret, in his book *Bennington Pottery and Porcelain*, illustrates this jug beside its Bennington copy. The more slender neck identifies it as the English version. See chapter on Reproductions. Mr Barret states that the design for 'Snowdrop' (his title) was taken from a painting or illustration by the artist Mr Henry Fitz Cook.

Height: 5¹/₂ inches
Impressed: **30**
Impressed: **1**
Impressed inside a wreath: **J. Dimmock & Co Harvey**
From the Morpeth Collection

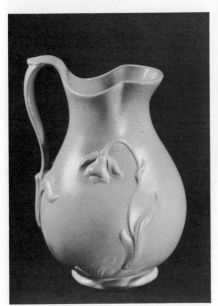

161
'International'
William Brownfield 25 January 1862

Four fields of endeavour are illustrated here in panels surrounded by stylized strapwork. Science, art, music and commerce are represented by classical figures using the tools of the given endeavour. The blue and white parian body is in the typical Brownfield shape. Also found in white stoneware.

Height: 7¹/₂ inches
Impressed in circular band; **International**
Impressed: Registration Diamond
Impressed inside a Staffordshire Knot:
30
WB

162
Prince Consort
Old Hall Earthenware Co. (Ltd) Hanley
9 April 1862

The unusual aspect of Prince Consort is

the highly ornate handle which is topped with a crown. On one side of the white stippled stoneware body are Prince Albert's Coat of Arms, placed in a cartouche; the reverse bears a bust of the Prince Consort. The emblems of the Orders which he held surround the neck of the jug. A ball weight as mentioned in number 111 is used in this jug to allow the lid to close without assistance.

Height: 8 inches
Impressed: Registration Diamond with **OHECL** at the top
Impressed: **23**
Impressed: **21**
Courtesy of Richard Riley Antiques

163
Circular Hop Vine
Liddle, Elliot & Sons 16 January 1863

Circular-growing vines and berries surround a brown stippled stoneware background. It is likely that this stippling was used to cover up defects in the body of the jug. This small neck makes an unusual shape.

Height: 6½ inches
Impressed: Registration Diamond

164
White Fawn
Beech & Hancock 25 April 1863

A shy white fawn wanders in the forest in a bright green ground earthenware body.

Height: 7³/₄ inches
Impressed: Registration Diamond

Height: 7 inches
Impressed: Registration Diamond
Impressed in a circular band:
Albion 24 Cobridge WB
From the Morpeth Collection

166
'Pansy'
W. T. Copeland 13 February 1864

165
'Albion'
William Brownfield 14 October 1863

This light-blue stoneware jug commemorates the wedding of Edward, Prince of Wales, and Alexandra, Princess of Denmark, on 10 March 1863 in Windsor at St George's Chapel. The arms are those of Prince Edward and the Danish Royal Family. In order to properly display these arms on the jug, Brownfield made a departure from the usual shape of his jugs using a more bulbous design. The jug has a twisted rope handle.

Pansies grow in a naturalistic form on the white stoneware jug.

Height: 8½ inches
Impressed: Registration Diamond with
 Copeland above, **18** below
From the Morpeth Collection

167
Corncob
T. C. Brown – Westhead Moore and
Co., Hanley 21 April 1864

A corncob completely covers this green stoneware jug, with the husks of the ear forming a handle.

Height: 6½ inches
Impressed: Registration Diamond
Impressed: **36**
 17

168
'Argos'
William Brownfield 29 April 1864

A blue stoneware jug with stylized anthemion under strapwork. The Greek

Key pattern surrounds the top under the metal lid. As in most Brownfield jugs, this example was done in many different combinations of colour.

Height: 8 inches
Impressed: Registration Diamond
Impressed inside Staffordshire Knot:
 W.B. Argos 24

169
Stylized Flowers
Hope & Carter Burslem
29 November 1864

White stylized flowers are on a brown stippled stoneware body with a band of stylized flowers around the top and bottom of the jug.

Printed: No. 2886
Impressed: Registration Diamond
From a private collection

Embossed: The Brownfield double circle bearing the words **Tiverton**, **Cobridge** and the initials **W. B.**, plus the size number **12**
Impressed: Registration Diamond inside the circle

171
Barrel and Grapes
Unknown c. 1865

This white parian jug is in the shape of a barrel with a bunch of grapes extending on to it from the grape vine handle.

Height: 3³/₄ inches
Unmarked

170
'Tiverton'
William Brownfield 30 October 1865

A blue stippled ground has an all-over decoration of white stylized flowers, vines and leaves.

Height: 8 inches

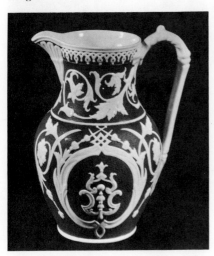

172
Calla Lily and Wire
Unknown c. 1865

A design of twisted wire covers the body of this grey-green stoneware jug. On each side a lily plant runs the entire height of the jug.

Height: 8 inches
Unmarked

Height: 8¼ inches
Impressed: **12**
            3

174
Stylized Anthemion
W. T. Copeland c. 1875

The pattern is geometric including white
stylized anthemions and strapwork on a
blue stippled stoneware body.

Height: 7 inches
Impressed: **Copeland**
            18

173
Medallion and Swags
Unknown c. 1865

The Greek Revival movement of
1750–1830 influenced every aspect of the
decorative arts, as well as the design of
this stoneware jug. A classical figure in
a medallion draped with swags is
pictured on either side in shallow relief
on a white stoneware body.

175
'Alloa'
William Brownfield 20 April 1866

This white stoneware jug is moulded in
the shape of a barrel with hop vines and
barley growing around the rim. The
name given by the maker, 'Alloa', defies
understanding.

Height: 8 inches

Impressed: Registration Diamond encircled by a band reading:
Alloa 12 W. B. Cobridge

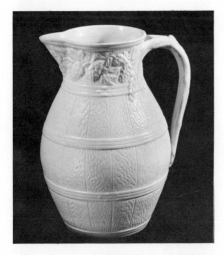

176
'Cashmere'
William Brownfield 15 March 1867

A white stoneware jug with formalized decoration in the shape of a tear-drop with stylized anthemion scrolls, beads, and diamonds. Also found in brown and

white highlighted with gilt.

Height: 8 inches
Impressed: Registration Diamond encircled by a band reading:
Cashmere 12 W. B. Cobridge

177
Hunt Jug
Ashworths 'Mason's Ironstone' c. 1867

An oval blue glazed ironstone jug in deep relief with the typical hunt scene of dogs making a kill, this time a wild boar on one side and a stag on the other. The tree branch handle extends into a band of leaves around the top of the jug. This design has been produced by Masons and Ashworths, now part of the Wedgwood Group, from early in the nineteenth century right up to the present. It is believed that this is a late-nineteenth century example.

Height: 7 inches
Unmarked
From the Morpeth Collection

was majolica and earthenware. This potter continued to produce his wares until 1951.

Height: 7¼ inches
Impressed:
G. J. Stoke on Trent moulded inside figure of eight cartouche
Printed: **12 67**

179
Arches and Scrolls
W. T. Copeland & Sons 24 July 1868

This geometric pattern features arches and scrolls in white stoneware with a metal lid.

Height: 8 inches
Impressed: Registration Diamond
Impressed: **Copeland**
G 24

178
Flower Garden
George Jones December 1867

Majolica ware has been made for centuries in many countries and was still popular in the third quarter of the nineteenth century. This bright multicolour glazed earthenware jug is a melody of spring flowers. Hardly any colour has been omitted. It was produced by George Jones of Stoke, whose speciality

180
'Club Jug'
Josiah Wedgwood & Co. c. 1868

A free 'running plant' designed grey

stoneware jug featuring hops and vines. The name 'Club Jug' was given by Wedgwood to designate jugs with this particular type of neck design. See picture. The impressed 'W' would indicate that the jug was produced in 1868, though the high handle would show an earlier date of design. Wedgwood continued to produce this jug at least until 1950, though a much heavier glaze was used on the later ones.

Height: 8 inches
Impressed: **WEDGWOOD**
Impressed: **W**
Godden's Mark No. 4075

181
'Westminster'
William Brownfield 21 October 1868*

A basket motif base with dark blue top in glazed stoneware.
Height: 6½ inches
Impressed: Registration Diamond headed by a ribbon impressed with **Westminster** and with **W. B.** at the bottom

* Although the registration symbols indicate a registration date of 21 October 1868, there is no such listing on this date in the British Patent Office List for Wm Brownfield. There is, however, registered on this date in the name of W. P. & G. Phillips a jug of this exact design.

182
'Ruth'
Cork Edge & Malkin
25 November 1868

Though registered in 1868, 'Ruth' is of very similar design to the earlier 'Infant Samuel' jug (see illustration No. 79) as it has basically straight sides, nipped in top and a cut-away foot. In two medallions it depicts the Biblical Ruth gathering grain. There is a stippled red ground. Without the registration diamond to date it, one would be inclined to say this was a much earlier stoneware jug.

Height: 8 inches
Impressed: Registration Diamond with **Ruth** incised at the top and **CE & M** at the bottom

183
Lambs at Harvest
Unknown c. 1868

A very large, highly decorative jug of white stoneware portrays on one side a child in deep relief with a tree branch around his neck and flanked by lambs

and a flying duck. On the reverse is a shepherd carrying a sheaf of wheat. Vines, leaves, and berries suround the figures. There is no lid though there are two holes where one should have been attached.

Height: 13 inches
No mark
Courtesy of Richard Riley Antiques

184
Pineapple
Minton Registered 23 December 1868

This is the Minton Pineapple jug mentioned in example No. 142. Again, the entire jug is the fruit and leaves of a plant, this time a pineapple. Majolica ware glazed in bright green and yellow makes an eye-catching kitchen jug. Also found in white parian.

Height: 6¹/₂ inches
Impressed: Registration Diamond
Impressed: **Minton**

Impressed: **538**
        30 16
Date code indicates that the jug was produced in November 1873.

185
Leaves in Cartouche
W. T. Copeland 15 July 1870

Cartouches enclosing two leaves alternate with stylized flowers on a white

body. There is a blue and white border at the top

Height: 8 inches
Impressed: Registration Diamond
Impressed: **Copeland**
From a private collection

186
Medallion
Cork, Edge & Malkin 22 July 1870

A geometric design of a series of four medallions linked horizontally around the jug on a stippled white stoneware. There is a metal lid.

Height: 7½ inches
Printed: Registration Diamond
C. E. & M.
    B.
Printed black mark: **Medallion**

187
Basket of Daisies
Unknown c. 1870

The base of this small jug is of basket motif in which naturalistic daisies are arranged. It is a white earthenware jug with stippled background. The metal lid is missing.

Height: 5 inches
Unmarked

189
Wheat and Rope
Unknown c. 1870

A white, highly glazed stoneware jug with tankard shape and metal lid. Upright stalks of wheat are separated by arches made of rope.

Height: 6¹/₂ inches
Unmarked

188
Persian
Unknown c. 1870

A white stoneware jug with Persian motifs on a stippled background. There is an angular handle and metal lid.

Height: 6¹/₂ inches
Unmarked

190
Lily
Minton c. 1870

This majolica jug comes at the beginning of the new era of design called 'Art Nouveau'. It is an excellent example of the sensuous new look which influenced the entire field of decorative arts. The main body of the jug is covered by rich green leaves surrounded by four white flowers potted in earthenware.

Height: 8½ inches
Impressed: **Minton**
  18   u
  1229
    37 Painted dark brown
  Date code **1870   m**

Height: 6 inches
Unmarked
Courtesy of Richard Riley Antiques

192
'Garibaldi'
Unknown c. 1870

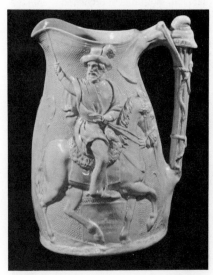

191
Graduated Rings
Unknown c. 1870

The body of this very plain tan stoneware jug is covered with descending graduated rings.

This large white stoneware jug is highly-glazed inside and out, an unusual practice for Victorian jugs. A larger than life figure of Garibaldi, the man who unified Italy, is astride a white horse on both sides of the jug. A placard proclaims 'Garibaldi, the Italian Patriotic Jug'. Rope is used for the handle which is topped by a helmet bearing the word 'Liberty'.

Height: 13 inches
Unmarked
Courtesy of Richard Riley Antiques

193
'Wedgwood'
Old Hall Earthenware Co. Ltd c. 1870

A very large white stoneware jug honouring Josiah Wedgwood, whose bust stands out in bold relief from a blue stippled background. He is flanked by the female figures symbolizing Commerce and Art. Next to Art is a pedestal holding Wedgwood's famous Portland Vase replica, then the seated figure of Science. On the reverse side from the bust of Wedgwood is a great

lion standing on a crown. Both Wedgwood and the lion are placed in a large tear-drop-shaped cartouche. Strapwork at the base proclaims, 'Wedgwood, born 1730 died 1795'. On the handle is a figure representing Fame. This jug is the ultimate in Victorian ornamentation.

Height: 10½ inches
Embossed: Circle with a rosette in the middle and the impressed initials **OHECL, Hanley**
Impressed: **16**

194
'Cupid'
William Brownfield & Son
14 December 1872

Two white cupids play in medallions on a brown stippled stoneware body.

Height: 6½ inches
Embossed: Registration Diamond with a ribbon underneath bearing the name **Cupid 30**
Impressed: Ribbon on top of diamond

Brownfield & Son on top of the
Staffordshire Knot

195
'Yeddo'
William Brownfield & Son
29 January 1876

A white oval jug with storks in relief on
a stippled stoneware background.

Height: 6 inches
Impressed: Registration Diamond with

Brownfield in a ribbon at the top and
Yeddo 30 in a ribbon at the bottom

196
Japanese Sprays
Pinder, Bourne & Co
7 November 1877

In the late 1800s, there was a renewed
interest in Japan and all things Japanese
which sprang from a Japanese Exhibition
in Paris. Ceramics were especially
influenced by this interest, and design
was infused with random shapes and
delicate flower sprays. This jug is an
excellent example of the Japanese
influence, as it features sprays of pink
cherry blossoms on a white stoneware
stippled body. Vertical grey bamboo
shoots surround the jug. The handle is
an irregular tree branch.

Height: 7½ inches
Impressed: Registration Diamond
Printed in black: **H**
826
Printed: **Pinder, Bourne & Co.**

197
'Hudson'
William Brownfield & Son
22 December 1877

Note how the neck and spout of this jug have flattened out and the handle receded below the rim, both of which are in keeping with the new form of the 1860s and 1870s. Three fishes swim together on one side, on the other a lone fish. The fishing motif has been continued by a fishnet design at the top of the stoneware jug.

Height: 7³/₄ inches
Impressed: Registration Diamond with
Hudson 12
 8 6/
    78 inside
Impressed: Brownfield Trade Mark with
Brownfield & Son impressed
See Godden's Mark No. 666

198
Swan
John Bevington 21 November 1881

A large white swan sits on the neck of a white stoneware jug. Two groups of large leaves rise from a footed base.

Height: 7 inches
Impressed: Registration Diamond
Photograph from the Public Records Office, Reference No. BT 43–73

199
Jubilee
James Dudson 1887

As is true today, any royal occasion in Victorian times brought forward all kinds of souvenirs in the form of jugs, mugs, etc. This blue stoneware jug was issued to commemorate the Golden Jubilee of Queen Victoria. On one side is a large bust of Queen Victoria with 'Jubilee 1837–1887' impressed in a ribbon. On the reverse is a bust of the Prince of Wales and his wife, Alexandra. Over their heads stands the three feathers emblem of the Prince of Wales and a ribbon bearing the words 'Ich Dien'. Below another ribbon says 'Long Life'. The base of the jug is surrounded by thistles, rose blossoms, and shamrocks to symbolise Scotland, England and Ireland. There is an example in the

Hampshire County Museum Service reserves.

Height: 7 inches
Impressed: Registration No. 66351
The number must have registered the shape of the jug only, for it indicates a date of 1850. The subject matter, Queen Victoria's Jubilee, demands an 1887 date of production.

200
Autumn and Winter
James Dudson c. 1895

A late white stoneware jug with a panel containing Greek classical figures on each side. The impressed 'England' on the bottom would indicate a date of manufacture after the passage of the

American Import law of 1891.

Height: 9 inches
Impressed: **England**
Courtesy of Richard Riley Antiques

201
Dancing Hours
W. T. Copeland c. 1895

The third quarter of the nineteenth century saw the end of moulded jugs as a distinct art category. It also saw the emergence of the true tankard as the most common shape for jugs. This has continued to the present day. The tankards of the 1890s generally had white moulded classical motifs applied to a dark glazed stoneware body rather than moulded with the body. They were simple, utilitarian and elegant. The illustrated jug shows a group of classical figures holding hands and dancing around a dark blue body. These figures, called 'Houris', are sprigged (moulded, then applied). The bowl of the jug is not moulded, but rather it is thrown and turned on a wheel. The beading is made

with a roulette-type device which pushes the clay up to form the beads.

Height: 7 inches
Impressed: **Copeland**
England
18
Godden's Mark No. 1076 Registration No. 180988
Printed: England

202
Mask and Dolphin
Unknown Twentieth Century
Reproduction

This is a twentieth-century reproduction jug. Even though there is no modern mark to warn of a reproduction, there is little likelihood one would mistake this jug for a nineteenth-century one. The poor moulding, high glaze, and strong blue colour all combine to indicate modern origin.

Height: 8½ inches
Unmarked

[114]

203
Miniatures
Unknown c. 1860

There are many jugs to be found in miniature size, that is, under two inches tall. Most commonly they are floral in motif and are usually found in various colours of parian. Obviously, the smaller the jug, the more difficult it is to find a clear, distinct moulding, thus it is very rare to find a miniature jug with a story-telling theme. Here is a selection of very small jugs found to date.

Height: 1½ to 2 inches
Unmarked
From the collection of Mrs John Adamson

204
Additional Designs

There were literally thousands of designs created and produced by the many companies which potted from 1830 through 1895. This digest lists only those actually seen by the author. The following is a list of a few of the undiscovered jugs recorded in the Public Records Office Design Registration books. The 5 and 6 digit number is that given to the design by the Patent Office, the date is the date of registration with that office. Reference: BT 43–65, 66, and 67.

(a) 55456 BLACKBERRY Minton & Co. 21 November 1848

(b) 87228 MAZEPPA THE COSSACK Wm Brownfield 25 October 1852

(c) 91406 JULIUS CAESAR Livesley, Powell & Co. 14 June 1853

(d) 97508 FEEDING BABY BIRDS George Ray 31 October 1854

(e) 99394 CUPID AND BOW Pratt & Co. 17 February 1855

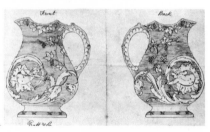

(f) 101623 SACRIFICE OF IPHI-GENIA Samuel Bevington & Son 27 September 1855

(g) 100624 'THE GRACES' J. Thompson 4 July 1855

(h) 103404 'HOME AND ABROAD' James Pankhurst & Co. 15 January 1856

(j) 112875 'HAVELOCK' Cockson & Harding 29 January 1858

(i) 103872 'HERE WE ARE' Richard Wynm Keene 22 February 1856

(k) 121724 'DANIEL IN THE LION'S DEN' Samuel Alcock 27 August 1859

205
Other moulded wares

Although moulded ware usually took the form of jugs, many other household items were made in the medium. A few examples follow:

(a) 3 piece butter dish, c. 1830 and unmarked in drabware.

(b) 17 piece Ridgway tea service c. 1830 in drabware.

(c) Tobacco canister in grey stoneware c. 1845 unmarked but possibly Charles Meigh.

(d) Tiny blue stoneware mustard pot unmarked c. 1850.

(e) Impressed Wedgwood mark white glazed stoneware tea pot with dog finial c. 1840.

(f) Don pottery teapot in the all-over daisy pattern unmarked.

(g) Davenport brown and white earthenware hunt mug c. 1815, which has been thrown and sprigged.

(h) Staffordshire tea pot with metal lid unmarked c. 1865.

(i) Drabware Ridgway toothbrush holder c. 1830 unmarked.

(j) 'Warwick Vase' Teapot
William Ridgway c. 1835
In 1771 a colossal marble classical vase was found in the Papal Territories of Italy. It was purchased and restored by Sir William Hamilton and sold to the Earl of Warwick. For many years the Earl forbade casts to be made from it. Eventually, however, it did become the subject of many replicas in every conceivable material. This teapot is not an identical replica of the Warwick Vase, but the motif for it was definitely taken from the Vase. The stoneware lid and body are generously decorated with

wandering grape leaves encompassing classical and animal heads. There is a two-pronged grape-vine handle. At some time in the past the spout has been broken and capped with a silver mount, an indication that the owner at that time highly valued his teapot. Ridgway gave this teapot the pattern number '6'.

Height: 4 inches
Unmarked
Courtesy of Richard Riley Antiques

(k) Birds and Bamboo
W. T. Copeland 21 January 1874

Another white stoneware teapot inspired by the aesthetic movement. Birds and bamboo stalks mingle on the two flat

sides of the teapot, which has a metal top and a bamboo handle. Also found highly glazed inside and out in various bright colours.

Height: 6 inches
Impressed: Registration Diamond
Impressed: **Copeland** below lozenge
Impressed: **18** above lozenge
From the Morpeth Collection

(l) Birds in the Vines
Powell & Bishop 26 January 1877
This white bulbous teapot with metal lid, typical of the aesthetic movement, is decorated with birds and vines in shallow relief. There is a Greek key type design around the base enclosing a leaf in each key.

Height: 6 inches
Impressed: Caduceus symbol
Impressed: Registration diamond
Embossed: Ribbon with the letters **HIZEN** inside
Note: 'Hizen' is a name given to a number of articles which have the Japanese influence.
Picture taken from the Public Records Office Code Reference, class 4, BT.43.70.

Appendix I   List of Potters

1   Samuel Alcock & Co.
    Cobridge
    Hill Pottery, Burslem
    Staffordshire Potteries
    c. 1828–1853
    c. 1830–1859
    c. 1828–1859

2   Bates and Co. (perhaps
    J. Ridgway, Bates & Co.)
    Cauldon Place, Staffordshire
    Potteries Shelton, Hanley
        Unknown

3   Beech & Hancock
    Church Bank Works
    Swan Bank Pottery, Tunstall
    Staffordshire Potteries
    c. 1857–1861
    c. 1862–1876
        1857–1876

4   J. & M. P. Bell & Co.
    Glasgow Pottery
    Dobbies Loan
    Glasgow, Scotland
        1842–1928

5   John Bevington
    Kensington Works
    Hanley, Staffordshire
        1872–1892

6   T. & R. Boote Ltd
    Waterloo Pottery
    Burslem, Staffordshire
        1842–present

7   T. C. Brown
    Westhead Moore & Co.
    Hanley
        Unknown

8   William Brownfield & Son
    Cobridge
    Staffordshire
        1850–1891

9   Copeland & Garrett
    Spode Works
    Stoke, Staffordshire
        1833–1847

10 W. T. Copeland
    Spode Works
    Stoke, Staffordshire
        1847–present

11 Cork & Edge
    Newport Pottery
    Burslem, Staffordshire
        1846–1860

12 Cork, Edge & Malkin
    Newport Pottery
    Burslem, Staffordshire
        1860–1871

13 J. Dimmock & Co.
    Albion Works
    Hanley, Staffordshire
        Unknown

14 James Dudson
    Hope & Hanover Streets
    Hanley, Staffordshire
        1838–1888

15 Thomas Furnival & Co.
    Miles Bank
    Hanley
    1844–1846

16 Robert Garner
    Foley
    Fenton, Staffordshire
    1733–1789

17 Thomas Harley
    Lane End
    Staffordshire
    1802–1808

18 Herculaneum Pottery
    Liverpool
    Lancashire
    c. 1793–1841

19 Hope & Carter
    Fountain Place
    Burslem, Staffordshire
    1862–1880

20 Stephen Hughes
    Waterloo Road Works
    N. Staffordshire
    1842–1851

21 Elijah Jones
    Villa Pottery
    Cobridge, Staffordshire
    1831–1839

22 George Jones & Sons Ltd
    Trent Pottery
    Stoke
    1864–1907

23 Jones & Walley
    Villa Pottery
    Cobridge, Staffordshire
    1841–1843

24 Liddle, Elliot & Son
    Dale Hall Pottery
    Longport, Staffordshire
    1862–1871

25 J. & T. Lockett
    Staffordshire Potteries
    King Street, Longton
    1835+

26 Machin & Potts
    Waterloo Pottery
    Burslem, Staffordshire
    1833–1837

27 Charles James Mason & Co.
    Patent Ironstone China
    Manufactory Lane Delph,
    Staffordshire
    1829–1845

28 T. J. & J. Mayer
    Furlong Works, Dale Hall Pottery
    Burslem, Staffordshire
    1843–1855

29 Charles Meigh
    Old Hall Works
    Hanley, Staffordshire
    1835–1849

30 Charles Meigh, Son & Pankhurst
    Old Hall Pottery
    Hanley, Staffordshire
    1850–1851

31 Charles Meigh & Son
    Old Hall Pottery
    Hanley, Staffordshire
    1851–1861

32 Minton
    Stoke
    Staffordshire
    1793–present

33 J. E. Norton
    Bennington, Vermont
    USA
    1850–1858

34 Old Hall Earthenware Co. Ltd
    Old Hall Pottery
    Hanley, Staffordshire
    1861–1886

35 Pankhurst & Dimmock
    Unknown

36 Phillips & Bagster
High Street
Hanley, Staffordshire
1820–1823

37 Pinder, Bourne & Co.
Nile Street
Burslem, Staffordshire
1862–1882

38 George Ray
Longton and Hanley
c. 1840–1850

39 E. J. Ridgway
Staffordshire Potteries
Church Works, Hanley
1860+

40 William Ridgway & Co.
Bell Works, Shelton
Church Works, Hanley
Staffordshire Potteries
c. 1830–1854

41 William Ridgway, Son & Co.
Church Works
Cobden Works
Hanley, Staffordshire
c. 1838–1848
c. 1841–1846

42 Ridgway & Abington
Church Works
Hanley, Staffordshire
c. 1835–1860

43 Rockingham Works
Near Swinton
Yorkshire
1745–1842

44 Sanford Estate Pottery Clay Co.
Wareham, Dorsetshire
Unknown

45 Josiah Spode
Stoke on Trent
Staffordshire
1784–1833

46 John Turner
Lane End
Longton, Staffordshire
c. 1762–1806

47 Edward Walley
Villa Pottery
Cobridge, Staffordshire
1845–1856

48 Josiah Wedgwood (& Sons Ltd)
Burslem
Etruria
Barlaston
c. 1759–present
c. 1759+
c. 1769+
1940–present

49 Worcester
Kerr & Binns
Worcester
1852–1862

50 Worthington & Green
Brook Street Works
Shelton, Hanley, Staffordshire
1844–1864

Appendix II   Statements of nineteenth-century pottery workers

These are statements taken from Staffordshire pottery workers in 1842 as found in the Scriven Report.*

No. 4 – Herbert Bell, aged 12, looks very pale and phthisical. (*Employed by Minton & Boyle, Eldon Place, Stoke-Upon Trent.*)
I have worked in this room 4 years as handle-presser; I come at 6, and leave at 6 in the evening; I live about a mile off; do not go home to breakfast; I go home to dinner; am allowed half an hour for breakfast and 1 hour for dinner; I work in the same room with my father; father gets so much a week piece-making; does not know what father earns; all I get goes to him and mother; have a mother and sister, one works at the china-works. I get no holidays; remember, now, that I get about five weeks in the year: a week at Martinmas, 2 weeks in August, and 1 at Whitsuntide; all the other boys get the same, and a day at Christmas. I get meat at home, and have clothes enough; I get a strapping sometimes; think I deserve it; father is good to me; have got a cough, have had it 3 or 4 years; feel it more in winter; I do not think the jumping on the moulds hurts me; feel no pain from it; I do not like it; I want to go into another room; I like potting; would rather be a potter than a tailor or shoemaker; I never do night-work. Master and overseer are very good to me; they never beat me.

No. 37 – George Bentley, aged 34. (*Employed by Copeland & Garrett, probably as a mould maker.*)
I have been a potter 22 years; with this firm 12 years. There are 4 rooms in this department, and 2 men; no children. We receive our models from the room below, and pass them on to the pressers. This occupation is easy and healthy. I worked for Mr Wedgwood before this. Thinks the system carried on here, and there, better than at most factories; their plans are better, and we are better looked after. I get 27s. per week, day-work; the modeller gets piece-work.

No. 49 – Thomas Shaw, aged 47. (*Employed by Copeland & Garrett.*)
I am the bailiff and foreman of these works; have been in the employ of this firm and their predecessors, the Messrs Spode, 30 years, as an overlooker 24 years. I

* Evidence taken in the Staffordshire potteries by Samuel Scriven, Esq. Children's Employment Commission. *Appendix to the second report of the Commissioners, Trades and Manufacturers* Vol. 2 *Reports and Evidence from Sub-Commissioners*, London 1842.

assist the cashier in paying the wages; the hands are always taken on, and sent away by one of the masters; they receive their wages in hard cash, and are paid every Saturday night. There are 454 men, 249 women, and 77 children, the latter being under 13 years of age. The premises extend over nearly 14 acres of land, all enclosed, and consists of 19 ovens, 272 working rooms, 19 slip kilns, 42 warehouses, and 33 other offices; all well drained by sewers, which empty themselves in running water and cess-pools away from the premises. We have one steam-engine of 45-horse power, which is applied to grinding clays, flint-stone, bone, glaze, paint, and other materials used on the works; it also drives 2 throwing-wheels, 11 lathes, and an engine for breaking down broken saggers for grog; it also drives 2 blungers, 10 sieves, and 2 stampers. There are no children employed in any part of this machinery, except 2 boys who regulate the throwing-wheel. All its parts are fenced off out of the way, except the drums to the throwing wheels. The boilers supply steam for regulating the heat of the green-house, throwing house, turning-house, and steam-house, or room for flagging plates and dishes. Some of the boys are hired by the masters, some by the men at handling, plate-making, dish, saucer, and cup-making, and by the dippers and oven-men, under no regulation of the masters. The men aforesaid engage with the boys, or parents of them, as to the amount of weekly wages – the amount depending on the inclination of the men; some encourage the boys by increased payments of 2d. or 3d. per week, over the agreement, for the boy's own pocket. I never hear of any case of cruelty or oppression, if I did I should immediately correct it. I think the greater part of the children attend the Sunday-schools, they are encouraged to do so. We have no school attached, or belonging to the premises, because it is a thing unheard of in manufactories of this description, and there are many evening schools in the parish, where they may attend if they have the disposition from 7 to 9 o'clock. The proper time to begin work is 7 in the morning; the doors are open at 6 for those who like to come and have fires to make; they have 1/2 an hour for breakfast, 1 hour for dinner, and if the trade should require them till 9, when in every case the doors are closed, then they have an hour for tea, making on these occasions 12 hours, otherwise their time is 9 1/2 hours; on the whole I think they work 10 hours; the children working with the printers work the longest hour; but Saturday they have the afternoon. The sexes are not much associated with each other among the children, the adults work together in numbers. We have separate places of convenience, and in no case do either sex interfere with the other. My opinion, with regard to potters and potters' children, is, that they are in as good condition as any others (not potters) that I have seen anywhere.

This factory does not, that I know of, come under the Factories' Regulation Bill; I do not know any workmen or factories that do, consequently I cannot judge of the working of that bill. I do not think that there is anything unfavourable to the health of the children in this employ, except in the dipping-house; some of the articles used there are pernicious, and if they do not keep themselves clean it is likely to affect their health. We have no washing-room for the specific purpose of washing or changing; but we have plenty of water and plenty of vessels to wash in, if they like. We have very rarely any accidents on the premises; during the 30 years that I have been here only two accidents from machinery have come to my knowledge; one occurred within the last 12 months, the other 20 years ago, when a man lost his finger; one or two from clothes taking fire; but not more for the space above mentioned. We have a porter at the gates whose duty it is to see the people come in and go out at proper times, and a watchman to take charge for the night as soon as the porter leaves. I do not know that I have any other observation to make tending to promote your enquiry, if any suggestion should occur I shall have a pleasure to convey it.

No. 95 – Charles Perry, aged 13. (*Employed by Joseph Clementson's factory as a mould runner.*)
I have worked for Mr Clementson two years, and run moulds for William Trowton all the time. I sometimes wedge clay. Can't read or write, never been to Sunday-school much; went to day-school for a little while when I was younger, and left to go to work. William Trowton pays me 4s. a week; we work regular six days in the week; master has always got work for us to do. I come sometimes at half-past five, sometimes at six, and begin to light the fire. William Trowton gives me now and then 3d. more than my wages if I am a good boy; he sometimes scolds if I am a bad boy, he never yet flogged me. I've got no father, got a mother, her's a painter by trade, but she's getting old. I've got one sister, and four brothers, all working as potters; we all live at home, and keep mother amongst us. I go home to dinner, and get sometimes bacon and potatoes. I have very good health, and like my trade, sometimes it is too heavy.

No. 99 – Ralph Bowyer, aged 38. (*Employed by Wm Ridgeway's factory, Hanley.*)
I have been a potter 31 years, with the exception of about three years; in the interval I was a publican and licensed victualler. I have always worked in the dipping department, or in departments connected with it. There are two boys working with me, – Samuel Cooper, and Joseph Hill, aged 16 and 11; the first has been a work four years, the other five weeks. I have three children, one boy, he is a dresser. I would rather not place him in the same work with me, if I did 'twould be because I could get nothing else for him to do, because I conceive that it shortens their lives. I have never been much affected myself, except now and then from a state of constipated bowel, and pain, numbness, and stiffness of my wrists; I have not the proper use of them. In holding the rough biscuit-ware between my fingers it denudes them of the skin, and makes them delicate, and even raw at times, when they bleed; I should think that the lead by this means is more rapidly absorbed. I have known boys suffer very much from this work; I knew two cases of fits and death to have resulted in boys working with me. I think children ought not to work here; the material is bad to work in, and the work is laborious as well. I work by the oven, that is, I have to fill the oven at a given time for so much money; the boys are paid by the oven too. I look after the boys' washing, because I know the consequences of neglect; I feel I should neglect my duty if I did not. I do not think we get sufficient pay for the risk we run; we have only 5s. per day.

No. 141 – Charles Cooper, Presser and Mould-carrier, aged 12. (*Employed at Thos. Furnival's factory.*)
I have been to work for Mr Furnival three years and a half as presser. I work for

myself; master pays me 3s. 6d. per week when I have that work to do; sometimes I only get 2d. spout-making. I can read, and write a little; there are four boys working in the same room with me, and eight in the next; very few of these boys can either read or write; we all come to work at six o'clock, and leave at six; never work over-time; I went to day-school before I came here; go to Sunday-school now; never go to an evening-school; I go home to breakfast, and get milk-meat, or broth for dinner; I do not care about the work, 'tis easy enough; I have sufficient to eat and drink at home, but have hard work to get it sometimes; father is a potter, and works with me; I have one brother; he makes cockspurs.

No. 175 – Robert Glass, aged 37. (*Employed by Messrs Meller, Venables, Pinder & Co., Burslem.*)
I have been employed in the potting trade 26 years come next June; first in the pottery, in Yorkshire, then at Southwick, in Durham, then at the Herculaneum pottery, near Liverpool, and lastly for nine years in this place and Tunstall. Until within the last two years I was employed in what is technically called the 'flat' branch, as dish, plate, and saucer-making as a workman; I am a workman now in the china manufactory, which is much less laborious than the earthenware; I have worked in the earthenware department with a jigger-turner and mould-runner; in this we could complete from 20 to 25 dozen of saucers a day, the dozen counted as thirty-six; that is, 75 dozen or 840 pieces in 12 hours or 1125 for 15 hours. The mould-runner has to run to and fro from the jigger to the stove with generally two saucers at a time, and this twice over, first to lay on the ware, and secondly for the polishing. I have always considered mould-runing in earthenware very laborious, much more so than in china, independent of running. I consider the excessive heat which he has to labour in, and the steam which is constantly passing off from the work, to be very injurious to his health; I think that although it does not produce deformities of the body, it nevertheless stunts growth and produces physical debility, such as to produce either premature death, asthma, or consumption; very few men live beyond the age of 45. In the dipping-house children working there are subject to injuries from the pernicious effects of the ingredients that are used in the glosses; but the proportion of children so employed are small, and the destructive properties of the glosses have been much modified of late years, yet its effects on some constitutions are even evident enough now. The treatment of children in some rooms from young 'prentices is oftentimes rough, and sometimes brutal; it arises from their capricious and lowbred vulgar brutality – the want of proper education. In the printers' department the labour for young girls is moderate, but they are made to carry water from the yards, by the women for whom they work, upon their heads; I have often seen them over-burdened. Those who are occupied in the most laborious departments are the lowest in morals; as a body, I should say that the poor little mould-runners are the lowest and the most degraded in the whole business of potting; the tendencies to immorality are various, but the main is drunkenness, and a want of the proper rational amusement to fill up the leisure time, together with a sound and consistent education. I have known many cases where children are obliged to fetch liquor for the working-men, and drink portions themselves, and are made to forage out the requisites for 'trimming a mess' during

drinking bouts; before I become more reflective, I regret to say I revelled in the like sin! They have been prompted to steal; I have known such cases where men are getting a hash, and wanted a few onions or potherbs, that they have been sent to the market-stalls to beg, and, if refused, have been told to watch the opportunity to run off with a bunch; they are commonly told to lie. There is a great evil in getting change at beer-houses: a common practice prevails with masters to pay one man for many others; a paper is given him, or a wage-bill, with the names of several parties and their respective sums for week's work inserted, which he carries, followed by his train, to some favourite public-house, or beer-shop, to obtain change, and appropriate. The standard custom is, if a man does not go with him for his wages, he forfeits 3d.; if he drinks his quota, well and good; others, better disposed, obtain their change of tradesmen, who get 1d. in the pound: by the former practice children imbibe habits of intemperance and idleness. There is very little encouragement to cultivate the morals of children or adults: manufacturers and foremen frequently treat with contumely those who have improved, or seem to have a desire to improve themselves; workmen look upon their efforts as affectation, whilst vulgarity and obscenity is tolerated and fostered. There are a great many who play on the Monday partially, and who work hard in the middle days; the boys work with them, and frequently continue to do for 15 hours a day: my opinion is, that they ought not to be allowed to do so; I believe it would be not only better for children, but a benefit to the manufacturer, if he closed his gates at six o'clock. I have worked in the several places named, and cannot say that I have perceived any very particular difference in the characters of children in the trade of potting: I can, however, see a difference in children working in the potteries, as compared with others not working in factories, and believe them to be in point of moral conduct and education below par. If I may be allowed to give an opinion of the cause of this deficiency, I should say that it resulted from the ignorance of the adult population; to remedy which it is only necessary to establish a good system of moral education for the rising generation, by establishing institutions in which rational and healthful amusements and industrial training was observed and followed out.

No. 212 – Elijah Hughes, Principal, aged 27. (*Employed by Stephen Hughes & Co., Cobridge.*)
I was born and bred a potter; so were my two brothers of the firm, as well as my father before us; we have, at a rough guess, about 170 people engaged in our works, amongst these a considerable numbr of children under 13, as well as apprentices, boys and girls, about 15; the apprentices we like to take at 14; they serve seven years; I regret to say that our indentures are but nominal: the consequences are that if a boy turns out badly he leaves our employ and shifts for himself, and no more pains are taken with him; he makes application at another factory for work; the former employers are informed of it; this is the understanding with us all, and we too, if we find out that they are taken to other places, inform the masters of his having left us an apprentice, when he is again sent away, unless he can obtain his discharge from us. I think if they were regularly stamped indentures we should take more pains with them, and get them forward in their trade; they sometimes defy us, and if we have occasion to take them before a magistrate for bad conduct he

discharges the case as the document is illegal. There are some thousands of children who engage themselves yearly to the works, simply by a form of agreement. If the stamp duty was reduced to 7s. or 5s. I would take none without it, and believe that others would follow the example, by which the government would derive a considerable revenue, and would benefit the children; it is a frequent practice with them, after they have served two or three years, and become half-perfected in their trade, for them to leave, and if they can get places elsewhere they do, thereby depreciating the value of the good journeyman's labour. It is my opinion that children ought not to be taken into employ before 10 years of age, they would then have the privilege of early education, which they cannot have now, and be much more healthy, and fit for their occupations when they come; they would be more likely to turn out eventually better.

No. 213 – Charles Bullock, aged 11. (*Employed by Stephen Hughes & Co., Cobridge-*
I am a runner of moulds for Absolem Stubbs; I cannot read or write; I come in the morning at six, go home at eight, six and seven. I get 2s. 6d. a week: father is an engine tender, always in work; mother stays at home; I have three brothers and one sister: one works at the pit, tother two go to school; sister is burnisher.

No. 214 – Mary Seadon, aged 46. (*Employed by Stephen Hughes & Co., Cobridge.*)
I have been a paintress since I was 10 years old; in this firm 20 years. I have the management of the girls' room; there are 13 under 13 years of age, out of these three cannot read; the rest can a little, and write a little; they all go to Sunday-school. My opinion of the general character of them is that it is as good as any other set; they are as well clothed and fed, and conducted well.

Appendix III   Glossary of pottery terms

Basalt   A black unglazed stoneware body developed in the 1760s by Josiah Wedgwood. It was very hard and easily moulded which made it suitable for potting both ornamental and teaware articles. Its popularity lasted well into the nineteenth century.

Body   The type of ware from which the piece of pottery is made, i.e. 'parian' body.

Creamware   A cream coloured earthenware body of high quality perfected by Josiah Wedgwood about 1740. It was inexpensive to make, light in weight to ship, and was rarely heavily decorated, which gave it a clean appearance. It became the most popular eighteenth-century body both in England and on the Continent.

Earthenware   A ceramic body made from clay and silica compounds. It is fired at low temperatures and is usually glazed to make it less porous.

Faience   An earthenware body glazed with tin oxide which is opaque and hides the colour of the body.

Glaze   A vitreous substance which covers the surface of the clay to make it smooth, hard and impervious to water.

Intaglio   Any figure engraved or cut into a substance.

Ironstone   An earthenware body patented in 1813 by C. J. Mason which is particularly hard, heavy and durable. It is very similar to stoneware. See stoneware.

Jasperware   A coloured stoneware body, usually unglazed, introduced about 1775 by Josiah Wedgwood. It is close grained and can be highly polished and worked with lapidary's tools. Colour is either on the surface only, called 'dip' jasper, or throughout and called 'solid' jasper.

Kiln   The oven in which pottery is fired.

Lustreware   A method of decorating pottery in which a thin film of metal is deposited on top of the glaze, giving it a shiny surface. The addition of gold results in red, silver in yellow, platinum in silver, and copper in its own colour.

Majolica   A tin-glazed earthenware developed in 1850 by Mintons. It imitated the earlier Majolica of Italy. In common usage the term means earthenware coloured with semi-translucent glazes.

Parian   A creamy white biscuit porcelain-like body, usually unglazed, made to simulate marble and to be a substitute for the biscuit porcelain of Sèvres. Because it was easily moulded into intricate shapes it was widely used for figures and jugs.

Pearlware   Earthenware body introduced by Josiah Wedgwood which is similar to, and often confused with, creamware. Cobalt was added to the glaze for whiteness.

Porcelain   A highly refined clay body usually white. It has been fired to a very high temperature which causes it to partly melt and become translucent. A perfect piece will ring when tapped.

Pottery   A generic term for anything which has been made of fired clay. In common usage it has come to mean any opaque clay item that has been fired at a lower temperature than that used for stoneware and porcelain.

Press moulding   One method for moulding pottery. See page 4, for a discussion of this process.

Queen's ware   Wedgewood's type of creamware named for Queen Charlotte who ordered a dinner set made from it. *See* Creamware.

Relief   Design on a piece of pottery which rises above the plane surface of the item.

Rosso Antico   Josiah Wedgwood's version of red unglazed stoneware, which was copied from the Chinese.

Saggar   Fire-proof clay boxes or containers which hold pottery while it is being fired, thus protecting it from the flames and kiln gases. Because the saggars can be stacked, many pieces of pottery can be fired at one time.

Slip   Clay diluted with water to a creamy consistency.

Slip cast moulding   One method for moulding pottery. See page 4 for a discussion of this process.

Smear glaze   A glaze for pottery which is very thin with little gloss. Often it was used on the outside of moulded jugs accompanied by a heavy glaze on the inside.

Sprigging   Decoration for pottery which is moulded separately from the article and then applied to it.

Stoneware   A clay body fired to an extremely high temperature (about 1300°C), which makes it very heavy and hard and impervious to water without the use of a glaze.

Toby Jugs   A pottery drinking jug. It usually takes the form of a seated man in a tricorn hat holding a pipe and a mug.

Transfer printing   Pottery decoration achieved by pressing soft paper on which an impression has been made from an engraved plate on to the article to be decorated while the oxide-stained oils acting as a kind of ink are still wet. This can be done either overglaze or underglaze.

Vitrify   To convert into glass by heat.

Zaffre   An impure cobalt oxide used to colour blue and white pottery underglaze. It produced a dark, opaque, cobalt blue.

Bibliography

Art Journal Illustrated Catalogue of the Great Exhibition 1851 and 1862.

Art Journal Illustrated Catalogue of the Universal Exhibition 1867.

Atterbury, J., *European Pottery and Porcelain*, Mayflower Books, 1979.

Barret, Richard Carter, *Bennington Pottery and Porcelain*, Bonanza, 1958.

Barret, Richard Carter, *How to Identify Bennington Pottery*, Stephen Green Press, 1964.

Bodey, Hugh, *Twenty Centuries of British Industry*. David & Charles, 1975.

City Museum, Stoke on Trent, *Stonewares and Stonechinas of Northern England to 1851*, City Museum, 1982.

Colliers Encyclopedia, P. F. Collier & Son, 1950.

Cushion, J. P., *Pocket Book of British Ceramic Marks*, Faber & Faber, 1959.

Durant, Will and Ariel, *Rousseau and Revolution*, Simon & Schuster, 1967.

Godden, Geoffrey A., *Encyclopedia of British Pottery and Porcelain Marks*, Bonanza, 1964.

Godden, Geoffrey A., *An Illustrated Encyclopedia of British Pottery and Porcelain*, Bonanza, 1965.

Godden, Geoffrey A., *The Illustrated Guide to Ridgway Porcelain*, Barrie & Jenkins, 1972.

Godden, Geffrey A., *Jewitt's Ceramic Art of Great Britain 1800–1900*, Barrie & Jenkins, 1972.

Godden, Geoffrey A., *British Pottery. An Illustrated Guide*, Barrie & Jenkins, 1974.

Godden, Geoffrey, A., *Godden's Guide to Mason's China and the Ironstone Wares*, Antique Collector's Club, 1980.

Haggar, R. G., Mountford, A. R., and Thomas, J. 'Pottery' in *Victoria County History of Staffordshire*, vol. 2, Oxford University Press, 1967.

Henrywood, R. K., 'The Moulded Jugs of William Ridgway and His Successors', and 'The Moulded Jugs of William Brownfield', *Antique Collecting Magazine*.

Henrywood, R. K., *Relief Moulded Jugs, 1820–1900*, Antique Collector's Club Ltd, 1984.

May, John and Jennifer, *Commemorative Pottery*, Heinemann, 1972.

Paton, James, *Jugs. A Collectors' Guide*, Souvenir Press, 1976.

Public Records Office, Kew, for registration of designs.

Scriven, Samuel, Esq., evidence given to the Children's Employment Commission, *Appendix to the Second Report of the Commissioners, Traders and Manufacturers*, Vol. 2, *Reports and Evidence from Sub-Commissioners*, London, 1842.

Shinn, Charles and Dorrie, *Victorian Parian China*, Barrie & Jenkins, 1971.

Smith, Alan, *The Illustrated Guide to Herculaneum 1796–1840*, Barrie & Jenkins, 1970.

Wakefield, Hugh, *Victorian Pottery*, Barrie & Jenkins, 1962.

Index by jug title

Index by maker

Alcock, Samuel
  'Arabic' 74, 'Ariadne' 87, 'Aristo' 90, 'Babes in the Woods' 59, Battle of Acre 58, Cain and Abel 89,Camel 86, 'Distin Family' 60, Flowers among Barley 88, 'Gipsey' (sic) 47a, Horizontal Grape Vine 116, Ivy Leaf 115, 'Naomi' 73, 'Portland Vase' 56, 'Wisdom and Providence' 57

Bates & Co.
  Pine Cone 142

Beech & Hancock
  White Fawn 164

Bell, J. & M. P. and Co.
  'Vintage' 126

Bevington, John
  Swan 198

Boote, T. & R.
  'Death of Sir Robert Peel' 85, Infant Samuel 79

Brown, T. C.
  Corncob 167

Brownfield,William
  'Albion' 165, 'Alloa' 175, 'Argos' 168, 'Cashmere' 176, 'Fern' 138, Gothic Ivy 134, 'International' 161, Scrolls and Flowers 140, 'Swiss' 131, 'Tiverton' 170, 'Union' 159, 'Westminster' 181, 'Yeddo' 195

Brownfield, William & Son
  'Cupid' 194, 'Hudson' 197

Copeland, W. T. & Sons Ltd
  Arches and Scrolls 179, Dancing Hours 163, 'Hops Jug' 118, 'The Jolly Toper' 99, Leaves in Cartouche 185, Lily of the Valley 82, Musical Instruments 130, 'Nymphea' 103 Other moulded ware: Birds and Bamboo Teapot 205k, 'Pansy' 166, Stylised Anthemion 174, 'The Vintage' 100

Copeland & Garrett, late Spode
  Classical Dancers 201, Wedding at Gretna Green 61, Vintage 70a, Youth and Old Age 62

Cork & Edge
  'Babes in the Woods' (probably) 129, 'Ino' (probably) 128

Cork, Edge & Malkin
  Basketweave 157, Medallion 186, 'Ruth' 182

Davenport
  Other moulded ware: Hunt Mug 205g

Dimmock, J. & Co.
  'Harvey' 160

Don Pottery
  Other moulded ware:Daisy Teapot 205f

Dudson, James
  Autumn and Winter 200, Jubilee 199, New Pineapple 150, Pineapple 122, Wheatsheaf 145

Furnival, Thomas & Co.
  Falstaff 53,

Garner, Robert
  'Fair Hebe' 1

Harley, Thomas
  Satyr Mask 4

Herculaneum, Liverpool
  Marbelised Classical 5

Hope & Carter
  Stylised Flowers 169

Hughes, Stephen
  'Stag' 41, 'Stag' with Lid 41a

Hughes, Stephen & Co.
  'Robinson Crusoe' 114

Jones, Elijah
  Coral 23, 'Elizabethan' 33, Vertical Leaves 30

Jones, George
  Flower Garden 178

Jones & Walley
  'Gipsey' (sic) 47, Good Samaritan 44

Liddle, Elliot & Sons
  Circular Hop Vine 163

Lockett, J. & T.
  Bacchanalian Cherubs 109

Machin & Potts
  'Robert Burns' 22

Mason's Ironstone
  Boar and Stag Hunt 55, Falstaff 11, Hunt Jug 177, Silenus 37b, 'Toho' 54

Mason's Patent Ironstone
  Nesting Birds 49

A Collector's Guide to Nineteenth-Century Jugs

I would like to invite you to join a moulded jug collector's club, the main purpose of which would be the exchange of information about jugs in our various collections.

This book, in which you find this invitation, discusses approximately 200 different patterns of moulded jugs. There are another 150 patterns which subsequently have come into my hands and which I have identified by make and date. In addition there are 50 patterns on which I am still working. Many of you probably have marked examples of some of these unidentified jugs.

It is planned to issue a newsletter bi-monthly for the first year. Each letter will be in three parts as follows:

1. Identification of jugs in my possession which have not been covered in this book.
2. Input of information from readers.
3. A buy, sell or exchange column (I will not enter into the exchange either financially or physically but rather will put the two interested parties in touch with each other).

If there is sufficient interest, we shall organize a formal club and meet occasionally to view collections and to exchange information. There will be a charge of £8.00/$12.00 to cover the costs of publishing the newsletter for the first year. If you are interested, please complete the postcard overleaf.